盜火劇團〔華文劇本Lab〕I

Voleur du Feu Theatre [Sinophone Play Lab] I

目錄

出版序

　　戲劇這門藝術所反映的，是當下時空人們之生存狀態，至於創作的載體，只要人類繼續使用語言生活，則無論戲劇「進化」到如何新穎的形式，終究還是得面對由語言轉譯成文字結構的「劇本」（即使挑戰文字的方式有很多）。劇本這個文類，同時存在於文學與劇場的領域，我們都知道，這是一門極小眾的創作形式，不但如此，在以中文寫作的華人世界中，就算是我們可以接觸到劇本，也大都是西方的經典劇本，華文劇本的生產可說是鳳毛麟角。

　　盜火劇團成立以來，以「華文原創」之精神陸續創作了多部作品，更創辦了第一屆「自己的劇本」原創戲劇節，其主要目的有二：首先是創造屬於中文語系的（文學/劇場）劇本，其次是劇本反映屬於華人世界的生活狀態與思維。這種在文化上，尋求自身主體性的建立，在台灣早期有林懷民老師創立的雲門舞集，要用自己的音樂、用自己的身體、跳自己的舞；或者八零年代「唱自己的歌」的校園民歌運動…等等，均為試圖擺脫西方強勢文化的影響，確認自身文化在當代全球化之下的立足之地。

　　盜火劇團這些年來合作的劇本，包括來自台港中三地，以中文書寫的劇作家，創作的過程大都是劇作家親自參與排練，讓劇本可以從劇作家腦海醞釀、文字結構生成之外，還有演出前的排練場修改，以期讓劇本真正成為，可以適合搬演的文本。而今天，我們更跨出一步，精選了盜火劇團駐團編劇劉天涯的兩個劇本，以中英兩種語言出版，試圖將此實驗的部分成果，與本地及海外的劇場文學愛好者分享。

　　《那邊的我們》是2016年盜火劇團紀念貝克特110歲誕辰，由本人所策展的「生存異境」的下半場。劇作者舉重若輕，兩個角色嬰兒般的語言，看似家家酒的孩童遊戲，卻意外洩漏出殘酷的生命實相。劇中透過一對不願長大的哥哥，和一直長大的妹妹，兄妹兩人不斷發生荒謬可笑的戲劇情境，探討「我們從何處來？我們是誰？我們往何處去？」此一人類永恆的主題。

　　《姊妹》是2016年本人所策展的第一屆「自己的劇本」原創戲劇節中的四個作品之一，劇作家以愛德華‧孟克（Edvard Munch）的畫作《吶喊》為意象，敘述一對十年未見面的姊妹，某日，旅居國外的畫家姐姐，返台探望一直住在老家的超市收銀員妹妹的故事；劇情發展是時空人物不中斷的一鏡到底，在姊妹兩個角色陌生又熟悉的對話中，逐漸剝開隱藏在彼此心中，關於一幅畫、關於一盒麻糬、關於這個家…，既深邃又日常的生命秘密。

　　這兩個劇本使用的均是日常生活的語言，前者以幼稚化的簡單語彙，借荒謬劇場的形式，提出具有當代性的存在質問；後者以極端寫實的日常生活語言，處理在時間的流逝中，兩位女性（姊妹）角色之於家（父權），複雜幽微的心理情境。形式上，兩個劇本簡單通俗、面對大眾，並兼具社會性的哲學思考，更具有開發劇場實驗與創新之企圖與勇氣。

　　希望這個劇本集的出版，能夠對於華文劇場的劇本樣貌，增添少許色彩，並且更能夠將華文劇本的力量，推廣到海外更多不同文化的劇場世界。

團長/藝術總監　謝東寧

「在日落之前，

我好想再寫兩封信。

一封寄給外婆，

一封寄給天堂。」

僅以此書，獻給我至愛的家人。

《那邊的我們》

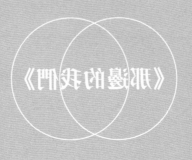

《那邊的我門》

角色

哥哥

妹妹

男子

老人

第一場

（燈亮，包著紙尿褲的哥哥和妹妹躺在小床上。）

（哥哥打哈欠，妹妹也打哈欠，兩人睜開眼睛，互相望一下，又把視線移開。）

（哥哥放屁，妹妹也放屁。）

（沉默。）

（哥哥打噴嚏，妹妹看他，把視線移開。很久之後，妹妹也打噴嚏。哥哥看她，把視線移開。）

（片刻後，哥哥開始吸自己的大拇指，妹妹也學他吸了起來。）

哥哥 （把大拇指從嘴巴裡拿出來）喂，妳是誰啊？

妹妹 （把大拇指從嘴巴裡拿出來）喂，你是誰啊？

哥哥 妳為什麼吸自己的大拇指？

妹妹 你為什麼吸自己的大拇指？

（哥哥不理妹妹，片刻後，開始吸自己的大腳趾，妹妹也學他吸了起來。）

哥哥 （把大腳趾從嘴巴裡拿出來）喂，妳為什麼吸自己的大腳趾？

妹妹 （把大腳趾從嘴巴裡拿出來）喂，你為什麼吸自己的大腳趾？

哥哥 喂，妳是誰啊？幹嘛學我說話？

妹妹 喂，那你又是誰啊？

哥哥 妳先回答。

妹妹 你先回答。

哥哥 妳先。

妹妹 你先。

哥哥 妳先。

妹妹 你先你先你你先你先。

哥哥 好吧，其實我不知道我是誰。

妹妹 太好了！太好了！

哥哥 好什麼？

妹妹 ……因為我也不知道。

哥哥 這裡是不是只有我和妳？

妹妹 我想是的。你是什麼時候到這裡來的？

哥哥 昨天…前天？還是一百天前？我不記得了。

妹妹 太好了！太好了！

哥哥 好什麼？

妹妹 ……因為我也不記得了。

哥哥 妳從哪裡來？

妹妹 你從哪裡來？

哥哥 好像有一條長長的管道，從裡面通到外面。

妹妹 一條很暗很暗的管道。

哥哥 對對！暗到我都看不到自己肚臍上的帶子了。

妹妹 一條很狹窄的管道。

哥哥 窄到我的頭和屁股都被擠痛了。

妹妹 到處都是水，真糟糕。

哥哥 我的手腳都舒展不開，只好把自己縮成一團，像這樣。（哥哥縮起來）

妹妹 對，就像這樣！（妹妹縮起來）

（哥哥和妹妹一起大笑。）

哥哥 然後突然間，我頭朝下，唰地一聲。

妹妹 從管道小小的出口被拉了出來。

（哥哥和妹妹滾下小床。）

哥哥 好亮。

妹妹 哇，好大，我的手和腳都可以伸展了。

哥哥 我就是這樣來到這裡的。

妹妹 我也是。

哥哥 原來我們是從同一個地方來的。

妹妹 原來我們來這裡之前，就是在一起的。

哥哥 妳知道自己長什麼樣子嗎？

妹妹 我不知道，（沉默片刻，指哥哥的眼睛）可是我從你這裡，可以看到我自
己。

哥哥 我也是。

（他們看著彼此的眼睛很久。）

哥哥 我應該和妳長得一樣。

妹妹 我也這麼覺得。

哥哥 我們長得真不錯。

妹妹 是啊。

哥哥 我好像有點開始喜歡我自己了。

妹妹 我也是。

哥哥 我和妳是一樣的，我喜歡自己，就是喜歡妳。

妹妹 是啊。

哥哥 我好像有點開始喜歡妳了。

妹妹 我也是。

哥哥 那我允許妳吸自己的大拇指了。（爬回小床）

妹妹 噢耶！（爬回小床）那我也允許你吸自己的大腳趾。

（妹妹開始吸自己的大拇指。哥哥看了一下自己的大腳趾，還是吸自己的大拇指。）

妹妹 （把手指給哥哥）給你。

哥哥 幹嘛？

妹妹 嚐嚐看跟自己的有什麼不一樣。

（哥哥努力地把頭伸過去，妹妹努力地把手伸過去，可是兩個人搆不到彼此。）

（妹妹把自己的大腳趾伸過去，哥哥搆不到。）

（哥哥把自己的大腳趾伸過去，妹妹搆不到。二人跌倒。）

哥哥 哎，沒關係。

妹妹 算了。

（他們吸自己的大拇指。）

妹妹 我餓了。

哥哥 吸自己的大拇指就不會餓了。

妹妹 我餓了，我想哭一下。

哥哥 不行！妳一哭，就會有人發現我們！

妹妹 我要哭了。

哥哥 那個人會把妳帶走的！

妹妹 可是我真的好餓！

哥哥 妳如果走了，這裡只剩下我一個，妳也只會剩下妳一個了。

（二人互看、點頭。）

（妹妹忍不住、大哭。哥哥驚慌地吸他的大拇指。燈暗。）

（燈再亮，場上只剩下哥哥一個人。哥哥吸大拇指。哥哥打哈欠，哥哥放屁，哥哥打噴嚏。）

（燈暗。）

（燈再亮，妹妹回到場上。）

哥哥 妳回來了！

妹妹 我回來了。

哥哥 妳去了很久。

妹妹 是嗎？我不記得了。

哥哥 從現在開始，妳會一直待在這裡的吧？

妹妹 呃…我不知道。

哥哥 妳如果走了，這裡只剩下我一個，妳也只會剩下妳一個了。

妹妹 …這裡不是只有我們兩個。

哥哥 妳怎麼知道？

妹妹 我剛剛被帶到別的地方了。

哥哥 別的地方？那裡有什麼？

妹妹 那邊有好多好多的玻璃房子，每間玻璃房子裡都有一張小床，跟我和你的小床一模一樣。

哥哥 真的嗎？

妹妹 那些小床上，睡著好多我和你。

哥哥 那邊的我們在做什麼？

妹妹 也在吸他們的大拇指啊！

（二人笑。）

哥哥 我們和那邊的我們，也都是從同一個地方來的嗎？

妹妹 我不知道。因為我看到了很多奇奇怪怪的我。

哥哥 哪裡奇怪？

妹妹 我看到有七個腳趾的我，只有一條手臂的我，還有身體連在一起的兩個我喔。

哥哥 啊，那邊的我們好可怕！

妹妹 不會呀，我覺得他們也很可愛，我也想和他們做朋友。

哥哥 怎麼會！好恐怖！…喔，還好，我跟妳，我們是一樣的。

妹妹 我剛剛在那邊，還聽到很多其他這裡沒有的聲音。

哥哥 什麼聲音？

妹妹 叭叭——轟隆轟隆，轟隆轟隆——滴滴——嗚嗚，哦咿哦咿…

哥哥 吵死啦，閉嘴…這是什麼啊？

妹妹 我不知道，可是我覺得很好玩。

哥哥 一點也不好玩，這聲音好恐怖！

妹妹 哦咿哦咿…

哥哥 閉嘴啦！

（妹妹沉默。）

妹妹 可以打開你的紙尿褲嗎？

哥哥 為什麼，我不要。

妹妹 我想看一下。

哥哥 看什麼？

妹妹 紙尿褲裡面的東西。

哥哥 …我不要。

妹妹 如果你不讓我看，我就哭了。

哥哥 不行！妳一哭，就會有人把妳帶走！

妹妹 那就讓我看。

（哥哥只好讓妹妹看。）

妹妹 哼。

哥哥 怎麼了嗎？

妹妹 我不知道我們是不是從同一個地方來的了。

哥哥 為什麼？

妹妹 因為我們不一樣。

哥哥 哪裡不一樣？

妹妹 你那裡有東西，我沒有。

哥哥 妳怎麼知道？

妹妹 我剛剛在那邊的時候，看到有那個東西的你，和沒有那個東西的我。我
們不一樣。

哥哥 所以妳要和我分開了嗎？

（妹妹沉默。）

哥哥 （把手指給妹妹）給妳。

妹妹 幹什麼？

哥哥 嚐嚐看。

妹妹 不要，我自己有。

哥哥 妳變了，妳不喜歡我的大拇指，妳不喜歡我了。

妹妹 我喜歡那邊，有好多東西是我不知道的，我想去看一看。

哥哥 不要去，妳走了，這裡只剩下我一個，妳也只會剩下妳一個了。

妹妹 你可以到那邊去找我。

哥哥 我不要，那邊那麼可怕，我要留在這裡，很溫暖，很安全，我還有我的
大拇指。

妹妹 那，再見了。

（妹妹開始大哭。哥哥慌忙吸他的大拇指。）

（燈暗。）

第二場

(燈亮，哥哥包著紙尿褲躺在一張兒童床上，吸自己的大拇指。)

妹妹 （從場外）哥哥！哥哥！

(妹妹上，頭戴蝴蝶結，身穿蓬蓬裙。)

妹妹 哥哥。

哥哥 （過了很久才反應過來）啊？妳叫我嗎？

妹妹 對啊！你就是哥哥，哥哥就是你啊。

哥哥 喔，我是哥。

妹妹 （沉默）哥。

哥哥 幹嘛？

妹妹 你為什麼吸自己的大拇指？

哥哥 …妳為什麼不吸自己的大拇指？

妹妹 因為那樣很蠢。

哥哥 妳不要忘了，從我們剛出生的時候，一起躺在玻璃小屋小床裡的時候，
 就在一起吸大拇指了。

妹妹 真的嗎？我不記得了。

哥哥 妳真的對自己很不負責。

妹妹 這麼久的事情哪會記得啊。

哥哥 我就記得很清楚。

妹妹 就算我有吸大拇指，也是人在小時候才會做的事。

哥哥 才不是。

(妹妹拿出電動開始玩。哥哥的注意力被吸引。)

哥哥 妳手裡是什麼東西？

妹妹 很好玩，他們買給我的。你想跟我一起玩嗎？

哥哥 不要，我沒興趣。

妹妹 可是很多和你一樣大的人都愛玩這個。

哥哥 我不喜歡，它好吵，可以請妳關掉嗎？我更喜歡跟我的大腳趾玩，妳知道為什麼嗎？因為它很安靜。

妹妹 你為什麼一直都像一個小baby一樣？

哥哥 我不想長大啊。

妹妹 可是你的身體跟我一樣大了，你不能再包著紙尿褲躺在床上了。

（妹妹把哥哥從床上拉起。）

哥哥 那我應該做些什麼？

妹妹 你應該穿你應該穿的衣服。

哥哥 我應該穿的衣服？

妹妹 在我們學校，那些跟你一樣大的人，他們都穿制服，戴黃色的小圓帽，筆直的黑色褲子，藍色的襯衫，背著書包，胸前還有一個很亮很亮的小牌子，上面寫著他的名字。他們都是很可愛的男生。

哥哥 …妳剛剛說什麼，我一個字也聽不懂。

妹妹 哥，你應該和他們一樣才對。

哥哥 那我問妳噢，穿那些衣服的時候，我還有紙尿褲嗎？

妹妹 哈哈，當然沒有啦！

哥哥 那我要怎麼拉屎拉尿？

妹妹 呃……這個…

哥哥 （躺回）我不要。

妹妹 為什麼？

哥哥 有穿紙尿褲才好。

妹妹 哎唷，那不一樣。

哥哥 就是一樣。

妹妹 不一樣。

哥哥 一樣！一樣！一樣！

妹妹 …我真搞不懂你，你是真的腦袋壞掉嗎？

（沉默。）

哥哥 ⋯誰說的？

妹妹 大家都那麼說⋯

哥哥 那妳覺得呢？

妹妹 ⋯我覺得⋯應該⋯不是⋯

哥哥 那妳還問。

妹妹 可是哥哥，為什麼別人跟你講話，你都假裝聽不懂，還在他們的身上尿尿？

哥哥 我沒有假裝，我是真的聽不懂。

妹妹 真的嗎？

哥哥 真的啊。

妹妹 那我講話，你為什麼可以聽懂？

哥哥 因為妳用的是嬰兒的話，是我們自己的話。可是他們已經忘記要怎麼講了。

妹妹 真的嗎？

哥哥 真的啦。

（沉默片刻。）

妹妹 怡兒費忒爆。[1]

哥哥 啊？

妹妹 德翁忙惹蓋爾克瘦思。[2]

哥哥 妳不要學他們！

妹妹 德啊昂歌航德伯奶。[3]

哥哥 不要講了！我要生氣了！

妹妹 哈哈，真好玩！

---

1. Il fait très beau. 今天天氣很好。（法文）
2. Tu veux manger quelque chose? 你想吃點東西嗎？（法文）
3. Tu es un grand benêt. 你是個大笨蛋。（法文）

哥哥 一點也不好玩。妳剛剛說什麼？

妹妹 我說，今天天氣很好，你餓了嗎，還有…你是大笨蛋。

哥哥 我不是笨蛋。

妹妹 哥哥，如果你一直這樣，以後再也沒有人會跟你講話了。

哥哥 為什麼？

妹妹 因為他們都不用我們的語言。

哥哥 哼，因為他們都把有意義的事丟掉了，開始對其他沒有意義的事感興趣。妳也是一樣。

妹妹 那什麼才是有意義的事呢？

哥哥 像我一樣啊，躺在床上，好好地吸大拇指。

妹妹 騙人。

哥哥 妹妹，妳如果再跟他們那些人一起鬼混的話，妳也會變成和他們一樣的，而我，身為妳的哥哥，會非常非常討厭妳。

（沉默。妹妹不開心地蹲在一旁。）

哥哥 他們之前是不是帶妳出門了？

妹妹 有啦。

哥哥 你們去了很久耶。

妹妹 沒有啦，就兩個星期。

哥哥 沒有很久？

妹妹 沒有。

哥哥 那有什麼好玩的嗎？

妹妹 當然有啊，你知道嗎，我坐了阿維嗡。[4]

哥哥 阿維嗡？那是什麼？

妹妹 阿維嗡就像一隻鳥，會載著你在天上很穩很穩地飛。

哥哥 鳥？跟我們家那隻每天在那邊嘰裡呱啦的東西一樣嗎？

---

4. avion，飛機。（法文）

妹妹 不是啦，哥哥，阿維嗡不是真的鳥，它是鐵做的，非常非常大，肚子裡面是空的，旁邊有一個一個的小窗戶，如果你從阿維嗡往下面看呢，（妹妹把哥哥拉起來，二人踮著腳尖往下看）樓房變得好小好小，人也變得好小好小，就像玩具一樣。

哥哥 好可怕，掉下去就死了。

妹妹 一點也不可怕，我覺得很好玩。

哥哥 還玩了別的嗎？

妹妹 我們還去嘎農呆⁵了。

哥哥 嘎農呆？那是什麼？

妹妹 ⋯哥哥，就像你現在在小床裡一樣，你想像一下，外面都是水。（妹妹搖著哥哥的手臂）然後你就會在水上漂呀漂，漂呀漂⋯四周靜悄悄的，只有陽光很暖和地灑下來。

哥哥 好舒服，我喜歡嘎農呆。

妹妹 哥，下一次你跟我們一起去家庭旅行吧。

哥哥 不要。

妹妹 為什麼？你對那邊一點興趣也沒有嗎？

哥哥 如果我在這裡也可以嘎農呆，那我為什麼要去那邊？

妹妹 那邊還有其他比嘎農呆更好玩的東西。

哥哥 我不要，其他的東西很可怕。我喜歡留在這裡，很溫暖，很安全⋯

妹妹 我知道，還有你的大拇指。

哥哥 對！還有大拇指！一起嘎農呆。

妹妹 除了我之外你就不想認識其他人嗎？

哥哥 不想。

妹妹 為什麼？

哥哥 妹妹，這世界上所有的人，都長得跟妳和我一模一樣，我只要呆在這邊，好好認識妳，好好認識我自己，不就等於認識那邊所有的人了嗎。

妹妹 才不是。他們跟你不一樣，跟我也不一樣。

---

5. canoter，划船。（法文）

哥哥 就是一樣啦。

妹妹 隨便你。我餓了。我要去吃東西。

哥哥 求求妳,妳如果走了,這裡只剩下我一個,妳也只會剩下妳一個了。

妹妹 我不會只剩下我一個,那邊有很多我可以和我玩。

哥哥 那我呢?

妹妹 你可以到那邊來找我呀。

哥哥 我不要!

妹妹 那你就只能自己一個人玩。

哥哥 我還可以和自己的大拇指玩。

(妹妹跑下場,哥哥繼續吸他的大拇指。)

(燈暗。)

第三場

（燈亮，包著紙尿褲的哥哥坐在床上看電視。傳來暴力卡通聲。）

電視 各位大朋友小朋友，大家早安，大、家、好！

哥哥 好！

電視 動動手，動動腳，準備好了嗎？

哥哥 準備好了！

電視 跟我一起來，1、2、3，go！

　　　有一天大清早／粉紅羊起床／

哥哥 有一天大清早／粉紅羊起床／

電視 一切都很無聊／一切都一樣／

哥哥 一切都很無聊／一切都一樣／

電視 很好，小朋友，記得了嗎？

哥哥 記得！

電視 自己來喔！1、2、3，go！

（哥哥開始唱。）

哥哥 有一天大清早／粉紅羊起床／

　　　一切都很無聊／一切都一樣／

　　　他非常生氣／因為天上沒太陽／

　　　他敲敲鄰居的門／

　　　鄰居打開門／看到他／對他說／

　　　啊／原來是你啊／粉紅的蠢羊／咩！！！

　　　鄰居哈哈大笑／覺得／很爽／

　　　下一秒鐘他的頭／被砸爛在墙上／

　　　粉紅羊提著槍／挨家挨戶敲門窗／

　　　全村人／都被他／殺個精光／

鏘鏘咚鏘鏘／英雄粉紅羊／

鏘鏘咚鏘鏘／粉紅羊真棒。

（哥哥大笑，在床上滾來滾去，電視暴力卡通聲繼續。）

（穿著高中生制服的妹妹上。）

妹妹 哥。

哥哥 妳回來啦？

妹妹 我回來了。

哥哥 妳去了很久。

妹妹 是嗎。我不記得了。吼唷，你又在看喔？

哥哥 噓。不要吵…

妹妹 你看了多久？

哥哥 我不記得了。嘿嘿嘿…

妹妹 哎喲…你在看什麼，快轉台啦！

哥哥 （看電視）…等一下等一下！嘿嘿嘿，快點，快點！……砰！耶！

妹妹 那隻豬的頭被打爆了啦！好噁喔！

哥哥 嘿嘿嘿…這個很好看的，（拍拍自己旁邊）來，妳可以坐在我的小床上，我們一起看。

（妹妹用遙控器把電視關掉。）

妹妹 無聊。

哥哥 幹嘛？

妹妹 不許你看了。

哥哥 為什麼？

妹妹 太雷[6]不能看太久。

---

6. télé，電視。（法文）

哥哥 太雷？

妹妹 自從他們買來太雷你就沒讓它休息過。

哥哥 噢，原來你叫做太雷喔。我一直都記不住它的名字。太雷你好。

妹妹 要我講幾遍。

哥哥 欸，太雷真的很厲害，那邊發生的事，上面通通都有。

妹妹 嗯。

哥哥 有些很好玩，有些很可怕。

妹妹 嗯。

哥哥 只要我一直看太雷，我在這裡，也可以知道妳那邊在發生什麼了。這樣我們就可以有更多的共同話題了。妳跟我在一起也不會覺得太無聊。

妹妹 嗯。

哥哥 這樣我也就不用離開這裡了。

妹妹 我就知道你要這樣講。

哥哥 所以就讓我跟太雷玩吧！

（哥哥用遙控器重新打開電視。暴力卡通聲繼續。）

（妹妹用遙控器把電視關掉。）

哥哥 幹嘛啦！把那個給我！

妹妹 不行。

哥哥 快點給我，聽到沒有。

妹妹 不，給。

哥哥 我從一數到三，妳不給我的話…

妹妹 哥我是為你好。

哥哥 1，2，…2了喔。

妹妹 你看這種東西會變壞的。

哥哥 3。

（哥哥撲上去咬妹妹的手，妹妹尖叫，哥哥搶回遙控器，打開電視。）

哥哥 嘿嘿嘿。

（妹妹把電視插頭拔掉。）
（哥哥再按遙控器，電視都沒有反應。）

哥哥 妹妹，妳把太雷怎麼了！
妹妹 你不能再看了！
哥哥 妳把太雷肚臍的帶子弄斷了啦！
妹妹 你在說什麼啦！
哥哥 嗚嗚嗚太雷死了啦它死掉了啦！
妹妹 不要哭了啦！
哥哥 太雷它人很好，它是我最好的朋友，都會一直跟我講話，不像妳，總是要到那邊去。把我一個人丟在這邊。妳為什麼把它弄死！
妹妹 它沒有死啦…哎呦，太雷它是不會死的！
哥哥 不管，我要太雷，把太雷還給我，不然，（怒吼）我就把妳的頭給打爆！

（二人沉默。哥哥又開始哭。）

妹妹 哥，你不要看太雷了，我在這裡陪你好不好？
哥哥 （停止哭）…真的嗎？
妹妹 真的。
哥哥 妳不會到那邊去了？
妹妹 不去了。
哥哥 （笑）太好了，太好了…好吧，雖然妳弄死太雷，我還是原諒妳。

（哥哥把頭放在妹妹的腿上，吸大拇指，二人沉默片刻。）

妹妹 …哥。
哥哥 嗯？
妹妹 今天我在那邊遇到一件奇怪的事。

哥哥 什麼事？

妹妹 今天長官來我們學校視察，老師讓全校的女生排成隊，做體操，給長官看。

哥哥 然後呢？

妹妹 老師讓我們每個人都穿制服，同樣的上衣，同樣的裙子，同樣的白色襪子。就是我現在穿著的這一套。

哥哥 喔。

妹妹 我站在一個高高的檯子上，帶領大家一起做。

哥哥 （認真起來）真的嗎，我都不知道妳會做體操。

妹妹 我會啊，我是全校做得最好的。

哥哥 妳可以做給我看嗎？

妹妹 幹什麼？不要。

哥哥 求妳了做給我看嘛拜託妳了。

妹妹 哎呀好啦！

（妹妹站起身。）

妹妹 我只做一次噢，你看好了噢！預備動作，1、2、3、4，2、2、3、4，3、2、3、4，準備開始。

（哥哥笨拙地學著妹妹的動作。）

妹妹 我們就這樣做著做著，每個人都穿著同樣的上衣，同樣的裙子，同樣的白色襪子。

哥哥 1、2、3、4，2、2、3、4，3、2、3、4⋯

妹妹 我做著做著，往台下看，大家都在跟我一起做，我覺得很驕傲。
我踢左腿，所有人都踢左腿。我舉右手，所有人都舉右手。

哥哥 1、2、3、4，2、2、3、4⋯

妹妹 天氣很熱，我在流汗，所有人都在流汗。我轉圈，所有人都轉圈，轉圈！

哥哥 （轉圈）轉圈！

妹妹 我跳起來，所有人都跳起來。跳起來！

哥哥 （跳）哇！跳起來！

妹妹 （得意）我好像可以控制下面的所有人耶！

哥哥 這比太雷好玩多了！

妹妹 我越做越用力，我越做越起勁，我把腳踢到我的頭那麼高！
　　　左手！

哥哥 左手！

妹妹 右手！

哥哥 右手！

二人 1、2、3、4，2、2、3、4，3、2、3、4，4、2、3、4…

　　（兄妹兩個瘋狂做體操。）

妹妹 到後來，整個廣場好像都是我自己。同樣的上衣，同樣的裙子，同樣的
　　　白色襪子。我發現，所有人的臉，開始漸漸變得和我一模一樣。

　　（妹妹驚恐地停下，哥哥還在繼續瘋狂地做操。）

哥哥 妹妹，妳為什麼不做了？

妹妹 我不想做了。

哥哥 為什麼？

妹妹 我想看看其他的自己會不會停下來。

哥哥 為什麼？

妹妹 其他的自己沒有停下來，她們還是繼續做。

哥哥 為什麼？

妹妹 我不知道，我覺得好可怕。

　　（妹妹發現哥哥停不下來。）

妹妹 哥，你怎麼了？…快停下來，不要做了。

哥哥 1、2、3、4，2、2、3、4…

妹妹 停…

哥哥 3、2、3、4，4、2、3、4…

妹妹 給我停下來，停！！不要做了！聽到沒有！停！

（哥哥沒聽見似的繼續做操，妹妹打了哥哥一巴掌，哥哥猛地倒下。）

哥哥 （搗住臉）喔！

妹妹 …對不起啊，哥。

哥哥 剛剛發生了什麼？

妹妹 沒什麼…

哥哥 嗷嗚…

妹妹 怎麼了？

哥哥 我的臉好痛，手臂好痛，整個身體也好痛喔…

妹妹 （沉默片刻）哥，我覺得你說的是對的。

哥哥 什麼？

妹妹 那邊的每個人長得都和我們自己一模一樣。

哥哥 所以呢？

妹妹 我也好想留在這裡和你一起吸大拇指。

哥哥 喔，當然可以啊，歡迎，妳只要搬一張小床來就可以了。像我們從前那個樣子。

妹妹 嗯。

（沉默片刻。）

哥哥 欸，妳可以繼續嗎？

妹妹 繼續？

哥哥 繼續做體操給我看。

妹妹 …什麼意思？

哥哥 我在太雷上也看到很多和妳一樣大的人在做體操。

妹妹 所以呢？

哥哥 每次看的時候我都會覺得很興奮，很激動，身體熱熱的。然後…然後，有個東西會在這邊，頂著我的紙尿褲。好好玩喔。

妹妹 …

哥哥 喔對了，我忘記了，妳跟我說過的，妳沒有這個東西。所以妳不會有這種感覺。真的好舒服噢。

妹妹 …

哥哥 我喜歡看妳做體操。可以做給我看嗎？拜託嘛！

（妹妹起身。）

妹妹 …我本來以為你不是這樣的人。

哥哥 什麼？

妹妹 我本來以為你還是原來那個躺在小床上，只會吸大拇指，一點也不懂他們語言的人。

哥哥 妹妹我跟妳講，什麼躺在小床上，我現在會側手翻了噢，是粉紅羊教我的，妳看，無敵風火輪！（翻滾）很厲害吧？

妹妹 我以為你真的很天真！

哥哥 什麼？

妹妹 你說的話，跟那邊的人一模一樣。

哥哥 什麼？

妹妹 那邊是個可怕的地方，這邊也是一樣。

哥哥 妳為什麼不高興？妳餓了嗎？（把手指給妹妹）那我把我的大拇指借妳吃，吃大拇指就不會餓了。

妹妹 我討厭你。

哥哥 什麼？

妹妹 我再也不想聽你講話了。（拿起書包準備離開。）

哥哥 妳要去哪？妳剛剛不是答應我再也不會離開我了嗎？（妹妹不理他）妳如果要走，把太雷還給我！

（妹妹插上插頭，把電視調到最大聲。暴力卡通聲繼續。）

妹妹 你看吧，看到死吧！（大吼）麥和德！[7]

（妹妹氣沖沖地下場。哥哥繼續看電視，笑了起來。）

（燈暗。）

---

7. Merde，他媽的。（法文）

第四場

（燈亮，哥哥一個人在場上，紙尿褲已經變黃了。）

（哥哥在床墊和枕頭上滾來滾去，發出怪笑，他滾到了地上，玩枕頭。）

哥哥 喔好累。

（哥哥倒在小床上。）

哥哥 哦喇，好臭！

（哥哥聞了聞自己的紙尿褲。）

哥哥 臭死了！臭死了！

（哥哥跟大拇指講話，拇指的聲音由哥哥自己模擬。）

哥哥 大拇指呀大拇指，她好久都沒有來了。
拇指 是的。
哥哥 你可以告訴我為什麼嗎？
拇指 我想是你讓她討厭了，你這個笨蛋。
哥哥 我要怎麼做她才能回來？
拇指 她不會回來了。白癡。
哥哥 我要怎麼辦？
拇指 你自己心裡清楚，不要問我。
哥哥 我要到那邊去找她嗎？
拇指 廢話。
哥哥 可是我什麼也不會。我要怎麼做？…喂，教我一下，喂？

（大拇指不動了。哥哥跟大腳趾講話。大腳趾的聲音由哥哥自己模擬。）

哥哥 大腳趾，大腳趾，她好久都沒有來了。

腳趾 …蛤？

哥哥 你可以告訴我為什麼嗎？

腳趾 …喔。

哥哥 我要怎麼做她才能回來？

腳趾 …呃…

哥哥 我要到那邊去找她嗎？

腳趾 嗯。

哥哥 嗯。

（哥哥剛想出門。穿著套裝的妹妹上。）

妹妹 哥哥，你怎麼這麼不乖呀，你想幹什麼？

哥哥 妹妹！（抱妹妹）啊啊啊&（@*&%#*——

妹妹 哦喲，好臭。哥，你回去坐好行不行。不要老是讓我操心！

哥哥 *#¥&&坐、坐，&*。

妹妹 對，坐好。

哥哥 啊呃呃呃#%@*#@，唔唔唔…

妹妹 你說什麼我聽不懂。

（妹妹幫哥哥換紙尿褲。）

哥哥 嘿嘿嘿…

妹妹 哥，我跟你講，我要去很遠的地方了。

哥哥 很…遠。

妹妹 對，很遠。

哥哥 阿維嗡！

妹妹 不是阿維嗡，哥，我要結婚了。

哥哥 啊？

妹妹 結、婚。

哥哥 結分⋯

妹妹 婚，ㄏㄨㄣ，結婚。不是分。結婚的意思，就是永遠在、一、起。

哥哥 唔⋯唔⋯（抱住妹妹）結分！結分！

妹妹 哥，我們不能結婚，因為我們是兄妹。

哥哥 嗚嗚啊啊%@¥#*啊啊啊⋯結分！

妹妹 我不能再照顧你了，因為我要去照顧別人了。不過別擔心，我已經找到
　　　　更適合你生活的地方，我明天就把你送過去。

哥哥 ⋯

妹妹 我會常常去看你的。

哥哥 ⋯

妹妹 唉，跟你說這麼多有什麼用，反正你也聽不懂。

（妹妹下場。）

（沉默片刻，哥哥跟大拇指說話。）

哥哥 大拇指，你聽懂她剛剛說的話了嗎？

拇指 當然聽得懂，智障。

哥哥 她要結分了。

拇指 婚。ㄏㄨㄣ。結婚。

哥哥 她是不是要永遠離開我？

拇指 你自己心裡清楚。

哥哥 是我錯了嗎？

拇指 不要問我了！白癡！

哥哥 ⋯你不要再罵我了！⋯⋯她不喜歡我，也不會喜歡你的！

（大拇指不動了。哥哥對大腳趾說話。）

哥哥 大腳趾，你聽懂她剛剛說的話了嗎？

腳趾 ⋯蛤？

哥哥 她是不是要離開我了？

腳趾 …唔…嗯。

哥哥 是我錯了嗎？

（大腳趾搖晃，發出表示否定的音調。）

哥哥 …謝謝你，大腳趾。

（哥哥撫摸自己的大腳趾，燈暗。）

第五場

（燈亮，妹妹和男子向觀眾的方向望去。妹妹甜蜜地依偎著男子。）

妹妹 你看。

男子 嗯。

妹妹 你在看嗎？

男子 我在看呀。

妹妹 你知道哪一個是你的寶寶嗎？

男子 嗯…

妹妹 你不會連自己的寶寶都認不出來吧？

男子 怎麼會，親愛的，我看到了，我正在很專心地看他呢！

妹妹 那你說，是哪一個？

男子 正在專心吸自己的大拇指的那一個。

妹妹 那個不是你的寶寶。

男子 啊？那是哪一個？

妹妹 靠窗邊的呀！正在睡覺的那一個！

男子 喔，我看到了！

妹妹 …你真是的…

男子 好了好了，我現在正在很專心地看他了。比剛剛還要專心。

妹妹 吸大拇指是一個很糟糕的壞習慣，以後要阻止我們的寶寶這樣做。

男子 都聽妳的。

妹妹 …你看，他多可愛啊。

男子 是呀。

妹妹 寶寶都是這個樣子，一睡起來就沒個完。

（沉默。）

男子 …妳知道嗎，站在這裡，讓我想到我以前工作的地方。

妹妹 什麼？

男子 塑膠娃娃工廠。

妹妹 …

男子 所有的娃娃都是從同樣的模具裡面做出來的，所以大家長得都一模一樣。

妹妹 為什麼跟我講這個？

男子 只是突然想到的。妳看，玻璃屋子裡睡著這麼多寶寶，長得都一模一樣，躺在一模一樣的小床里，包著一模一樣的被單，小小的鼻子，小小的眼睛，每個人長得都像我兒子。

妹妹 …剛開始的時候都這樣吧，時間久了就好了。畢竟嘛，世界上怎麼可能有兩個人長的完全一樣啊。

男子 真的嗎？

妹妹 …就算是雙胞胎，也是有不同的。

男子 妳確定嗎？

妹妹 當然了…看完了嗎，要回去了嗎？

男子 妳先走吧，我想再看一下我們的寶寶。

妹妹 …那你快點回來喔。

（妹妹下場。）

（男子沉默片刻。）

男子 你知道嗎，我做爸爸了。你知道哪一個是我的寶寶嗎？你也不知道，對不對？每個人長得都一模一樣，我怎麼可能知道呢，我連自己和別人都分不清楚了。只有看到和我一樣的人，我才會覺得安全。真可怕，如果我可以永遠和你在一起就好了。（男子伸出自己的大拇指）真希望我可以快點找到那邊的我自己。不是我的錯吧，對不對？可是要去哪裡找呢？有的時候，我真的好想大哭一場啊。

（男子把大拇指放進嘴裡。他看著觀眾。）

（傳來此起彼落的嬰兒哭聲。）

（燈暗。）

第六場

（燈亮，哥哥和老人坐在場上。）

（哥哥對大拇指說話。）

哥哥 喂，大拇指，你喜歡這地方嗎？

拇指 嗯…

哥哥 我覺得還不錯，我本來以為那邊很可怕，可是住起來，和我的房間也沒什麼區別。

拇指 只要有吃有睡不就可以了嗎，笨蛋。

哥哥 是啊，不過沒有她跟我講話了。

拇指 反正她講的話你也聽不懂。

哥哥 是啊，她已經變成和他們一樣的人了。

拇指 這都是你的錯。妳應該把她留在你身邊才對。結果你就這麼輕易地把她放走了！

哥哥 …

拇指 你應該繼續去尋找，尋找那邊的我們。這是你現在的任務。

哥哥 …我要去哪裡找呢？

（大拇指不動了，哥哥看到老人，連忙對大腳趾說話。）

哥哥 喂，大腳趾，你看到那邊有一個人嗎？

腳趾 …蛤？

哥哥 他已經在這裡好久了吧？

腳趾 …啊。

哥哥 他一定也聽不懂我們的話…可是我發現，他跟我一樣喜歡吸大拇指。

腳趾 …呃。

哥哥 我們一起去跟他打聲招呼好不好？

腳趾 嗯。

（哥哥把腳轉向旁邊的老人。）

哥哥 喂！（老人轉過頭看他）你看起來跟我很像。你是誰？你從哪裡來？……
（對大腳趾）算了啦，他聽不懂我們的話。

（沉默片刻。）

老人 乙系隨？乙慫拉拉來？

哥哥 蛤？！

老人 你系誰？你從拉裡來？

哥哥 你在跟我講話嗎？你聽得懂我的話？

老人 唔，他…他們都聽不懂了。

哥哥 哎唷。

老人 怎…怎麼了？

哥哥 好久沒聽到同樣的話了，我的耳朵有點不太適應。

老人 我已經很久…不講了。

哥哥 為什麼？

老人 我一講話，他們就餵我吃…東西，給我喝…水…水，幫我換…呃…呃…
（指自己的下身）

哥哥 紙尿褲？

老人 對！紙尿褲！或者讓我看…看…（老人向他正前方指著）你知道那個是什麼
嗎？

哥哥 我知道，那個是太雷。

老人 對！…我一講話，他們就說，閉嘴！然後…讓我看太雷。

哥哥 欸我也是！……她說，他們這樣做，是因為我的腦袋壞了。

老人 她？

哥哥 跟我從同一個地方來的她。

老人 唔。所以還是不講話，或者講他們的話比較好。他們就不會…打擾我們
了。

哥哥 你會講他們的話？

老人 是啊。

哥哥　你和他們在一起，過了很久嗎？

老人　很久，久到我快有點忘記自己了。直到有一次，我遇到跟我長得一模一樣的人，才重新又想起來。

哥哥　一模一樣的人？真的嗎？你是在哪裡遇到的？

老人　那個時候我很年輕，還在打仗。

哥哥　我知道！我在太雷裡見過打仗！

老人　我躲在一棵樹後面，聽到身旁子彈嗖嗖地飛。炮彈就轟轟地落在不遠的地上，震得我一頭一臉都是土。

哥哥　好好玩喔！

老人　不知道過了多久，我聽見有人喊，快衝啦！！我就跳起來，衝上去。可是我突然動不了了。

哥哥　為什麼？

老人　我發現迎面向我跑過來的那個人，他跟我長得一模一樣。

哥哥　哇，是那邊的我們。

老人　我往他旁邊看看，發現所有人都長得跟我一模一樣。哎呀，見鬼了。

哥哥　原來那邊的我們有這麼多啊。

老人　真可怕。漫山遍野的你跑過來說要殺掉你自己。

哥哥　好可怕。

老人　跑在最前面的我向我衝過來了。怎麼辦才好呢？

哥哥　怎麼辦啊？

老人　我是殺還是不殺呢，搞不好那個人才是真正的我。如果我殺了他，真正的我就會死掉了。

哥哥　你殺了嗎？

老人　…我殺——！

哥哥　死掉了，好可惜。

（沉默。）

老人　就在不久之前，我開車，經過一個長長的隧道。

哥哥　就像長長的管道那樣嗎？

老人 對。

哥哥 很窄,很小,黑到看不到自己肚臍的帶子。

老人 那是午夜時分,車子很少,我開啊開,開啊開,不知道為什麼,隧道突然變得那麼長,好像永遠都開不出去了。

哥哥 喔。

老人 開著開著,我看到前方隱隱約約有一群人。

哥哥 是誰呀?

老人 我把車停下,等那群人慢慢走過來,等到他們走近了,我才看到他們都穿著軍裝,看起來很疲憊的樣子,所有人都很慢很慢地走著,腳下一點聲音也沒有。

哥哥 他們長什麼樣子?

老人 他們看起來很眼熟,很像我認識的人。

哥哥 是誰呀?

老人 我打開車窗,像這樣子——對他們大喊。(大喊)喂!你們是誰——?

(沉默。)

老人 你們從哪裡來?你們要去哪裡——?

(沉默。)

哥哥 有人理你嗎?

老人 走在最後的那個人,他要離開的時候,轉身看了我一眼。就一眼,我認出他是誰了。

哥哥 誰呀?

老人 就是我殺死的那個人。

哥哥 長得和你一模一樣的人?

老人 沒錯,一模一樣。

哥哥 那就是你自己啦。

老人 我突然開始同情他。所以我就對他喊——喂!…要搭便車嗎——?

（沉默。）

老人 所有人都停下來，回頭看我。

哥哥 然後呢？

老人 大家長得也都跟我一模一樣啊！

哥哥 好棒喔！

老人 我發動汽車，頭也不回地開出了隧道。

哥哥 為什麼？

老人 我的車子這麼小，哪載得下這麼多人啊！

哥哥 你的運氣真好，可以碰到這麼多那邊的我們。

老人 他們都是我殺死的人。

哥哥 然後呢？

老人 然後我就到了這裡。

哥哥 殺人是什麼感覺？

老人 ……唔。我不記得了。

哥哥 就像粉紅羊殺了他的鄰居那樣嗎？

老人 蛤？

哥哥 我問你，你有槍嗎？

老人 曾經有過。

哥哥 如果天上沒有太陽你會不開心嗎？

老人 唔…沒有人會開心的吧！

哥哥 …有人曾經對你說過，你很蠢嗎？

老人 啊，太多人這樣說過我了！

哥哥 …你是粉紅羊嗎？

老人 那是什麼？

哥哥 你是粉紅羊，但是你自己不知道！

老人 或許吧，這個世界上我不知道的事情太多了。

哥哥 哇，你是英雄！

老人 很多人都這麼說我。

哥哥 哇。你知道嗎，我崇拜你很久了！

（沉默片刻。）

哥哥 （指老人的眼睛）我從你的這裡，可以看到自己。
老人 我也是。

（他們看著彼此的眼睛很久。）

哥哥 我應該和你長得一樣。
老人 我也這麼覺得。
哥哥 我們長得真不錯。
老人 是啊。
哥哥 我一直很喜歡我自己。
老人 我也是。
哥哥 我和你是一樣的，我喜歡自己，就是喜歡你。
老人 是啊。
哥哥 那我也是粉紅羊了嗎？
老人 是的。
哥哥 那我也是英雄了？我竟然成為我最想要成為的人了。

（沉默片刻。）

哥哥 我可以再問你最後一個問題嗎？你的紙尿褲裡有那個東西嗎？
老人 什麼東西？
哥哥 就是這個啊。

（哥哥讓老人看自己紙尿褲裡面。）

老人 我也有。

（老人讓哥哥看自己紙尿褲裡面。）

哥哥 哇——我們是從同一個地方來的！那你會永遠跟我在一起嗎？

老人 在一起…我們最後都會在一起。

（哥哥把小床搬到老人旁邊，和老人一同緩緩坐下。）

（哥哥把自己的大拇指給老人。）

哥哥 給你。

老人 幹什麼？

哥哥 嚐一下。

（老人吸了一下哥哥的大拇指。）

哥哥 和自己的味道有什麼不一樣？

（老人吸了一下自己的大拇指。）

老人 味道一樣欸。

（二人笑。）

（老人打哈欠，哥哥也打哈欠。）

（老人放屁，哥哥也放屁）

（老人打噴嚏，哥哥也打噴嚏，二人笑。）

（他們開始吸自己的大拇指。）

（燈暗。）

—劇終—

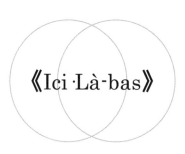

《Ici·Là-bas》

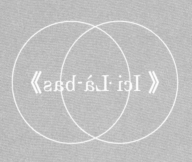

《 Ici·Là-bas 》

※THE CHARACTERS:

Brother

Sister

Young Man

Old Man

SCENE I

Lights on, brother and sister are lying in the delivery room, wrapped in towel.

Brother starts to yawn. Sister starts to yawn. They look at each other, then look away.

Brother farts. Sister farts.

BROTHER: Hey, what are you doing?

SISTER: Hey, what are you doing?

Silence.

Brother sneezes. Sister looks at him and then looks away.

Sister sneezes. Brother looks at her and then looks away.

Brother starts to suck his thumb. Sister starts to suck her thumb.

BROTHER: Hey, why do you suck your thumb?

SISTER: Hey, why do you suck your thumb?

Brother pays no attention to her.

Brother starts to suck his big toe. Sister starts to suck her big toe.

BROTHER: Hey, why do you suck your big toe?

SISTER: Hey, why do you suck your big toe?

BROTHER: Hey, who are you? Stop following me!

SISTER: Who are you?

BROTHER: You answer me first.

SISTER: You answer me first.

BROTHER:	Okay. Actually, I don't know who I am.
SISTER:	Great! Great!
BROTHER:	What?
SISTER:	I don't know who I am either.
BROTHER:	Are we alone here?
SISTER:	I guess so. When did you come here?
BROTHER:	Yesterday···the day before yesterday···about one hundred days ago··· I don't remember.
SISTER:	Great! Great!
BROTHER:	What?
SISTER:	Because I don't remember either.
BROTHER:	Where did you come from?
SISTER:	Where did you come from?
BROTHER:	There was a long long pipe, from the inside to the outside.
SISTER:	A very dark pipe?
BROTHER:	Yes! It was too dark, I couldn't see the string on my belly.
SISTER:	A very narrow pipe.
BROTHER:	I was jammed in pain.
SISTER:	There was water everywhere. Gross!
BROTHER:	I couldn't stretch myself. I had to huddle up like this.
SISTER:	Yes! Just like this!

They laugh together.

BROTHER:	All of a sudden, I started heading down.
SISTER:	Someone pulled me out of the pipe.
BROTHER:	So bright.
SISTER:	So wide. I could stretch myself.

BROTHER:	That's how I come here.
SISTER:	Me too.
BROTHER:	Ah, I see. We came from the same place.
SISTER:	We were together before we came here.
BROTHER:	Do you know how does yourself look like?
SISTER:	I don't know.

She points at his eyes.

SISTER:	But I can see myself from there.
BROTHER:	Me too.

They look into the eyes of each other for a long time.

BROTHER:	I look just like you.
SISTER:	I think so.
BROTHER:	We look great.
SISTER:	Yes! I agree with you.
BROTHER:	I'm starting to like myself.
SISTER:	Me too.
BROTHER:	We are the same. I like myself, so I like you.
SISTER:	Me too!
BROTHER:	I'm starting to like you!
SISTER:	I like you too!
BROTHER:	You can suck your thumb now!
SISTER:	You can suck your big toe!

Sister starts to suck her thumb. Brother takes a look at his big toe, then takes a look at his sister. After a while, he decides to suck his thumb.

Sister stretches out her thumb.

SISTER: Here you are.

BROTHER: What?

SISTER: Have a taste of it. Perhaps my thumb has a different flavor.

Brother strives for it but fails.

Sister stretches out her big toe. Brother strives for it but fails again.

SISTER: Forget it.

They start to suck their own thumb.

SISTER: I'm hungry.

BROTHER: Then suck your thumb.

SISTER: I'm hungry. I wanna cry.

BROTHER: Someone will take you away if you cry.

SISTER: I wanna cry.

BROTHER: If you go away, I will be left alone. You will be left alone too.

Sister starts to cry. Brother sucks his thumb with fear. Lights off.

Lights on. Brother is alone on stage. He sucks his thumb. He plays with his feet. He farts. He burps and makes strange sounds.

Lights off.

Lights on. Sister is back on stage.

BROTHER: You're back!

SISTER: Yes, I'm back.

BROTHER: You were away for a long time.

SISTER:	Really? I can't remember.
BROTHER:	From now on, will you stay with me?
SISTER:	Well···I don't know.
BROTHER:	If you go away, I will be left alone. You will be left alone too.
SISTER:	We are not alone.
BROTHER:	How do you know?
SISTER:	I was taken to somewhere else.
BROTHER:	Somewhere else? What did you see?
SISTER:	I saw many little houses made of glass. There was a little bed in each glass house, just like ours.
BROTHER:	Really?
SISTER:	I saw many you and many me on those beds.
BROTHER:	Us on the other side? What were they doing?
SISTER:	They were also sucking their thumbs!
BROTHER:	Do we come from the same place?
SISTER:	I don't know. Because I saw many me. They are strange.
BROTHER:	Strange?
SISTER:	I saw me with seven toes, me with one arm and me with two bodies conjoined with each other.
BROTHER:	Ah! They are so horrible.
SISTER:	No, they are cute. I also want to make friends with them.
BROTHER:	They are horrible··· I feel so lucky to be with you. We are the same.
SISTER:	I also heard many voices there.
BROTHER:	What kind of voice?
SISTER:	Beep Beep···Boom Boom···Choo Choo····
BROTHER:	Stop! Stop that! What are those noises?
SISTER:	I don't know. But that is fun!

BROTHER: That is not fun at all! That is horrible!

Silence.

SISTER: Kick off your towel.
BROTHER: Why?
SISTER: I want to take a look.
BROTHER: What?
SISTER: The thing inside your towel.
BROTHER: No way.
SISTER: I'll cry if you don't let me take a look.
BROTHER: No! Someone will take you away if you cry.
SISTER: Then kick off.

Brother has no choice but to kick off his towel.

SISTER: Well well.
BROTHER: So what?
SISTER: I don't know whether we came from the same place.
BROTHER: What?
SISTER: Because we are different.
BROTHER: Why?
SISTER: You have something there, but I don't.
BROTHER: How do you know?
SISTER: I saw you with that thing and me without that thing on the other side. So we are different.
BROTHER: Are you going to leave me?

Silence. Brother stretches out his thumb.

BROTHER: Here you are.

SISTER: What?

BROTHER: Have a taste.

SISTER: No, I have my own thumb.

BROTHER: You've changed. You don't like my thumb. You don't like me anymore.

SISTER: I like the world on the other side. There are many things that I don't understand. I want to go there.

BROTHER: If you go away, I will be left alone. You will be left alone too.

SISTER: You can come with me.

BROTHER: No, I want to stay here. I'm safe and sound here. I can stay with my thumb.

SISTER: Bye-bye.

SCENE II

Sister starts to cry. Brother sucks his thumb with fear.
Lights off.

Lights on. Brother is lying in a cradle with baby diaper. He
is sucking his thumb. Sister is sitting on the floor. She is
wearing a girl bubble skirt.

SISTER: Brother.

Brother didn't answer her for a long time.

BROTHER: Are you calling me?
SISTER: Yes, you are Brother. Brother is you.
BROTHER: Oh, I'm Brother.
SISTER: Brother.
BROTHER: Yes?
SISTER: Why do you suck your thumb?
BROTHER: Why do you stop sucking your thumb?
SISTER: Because that's stupid.
BROTHER: We were sucking thumb together by the time we
were born. Don't you remember that?
SISTER: Really? I don't.
BROTHER: You should be responsible for yourself.
SISTER: It happened so long ago that I can't remember.
BROTHER: I can remember that clearly.
SISTER: Human beings only suck thumb when they were
little babies.

BROTHER: Absolutely not!

Sister starts to play video games.

BROTHER: What's that?
SISTER: It's great. They bought it for me. Do you want to play with me?
BROTHER: No.
SISTER: But many boys of your age really love it.
BROTHER: It's too noisy. My big toe is a better friend, it's quiet.
SISTER: Why do you always act like a baby?
BROTHER: I don't want to grow up.
SISTER: But your body is as big as me. You can't stay in the cradle with baby diaper any more.
BROTHER: Then what should I do?
SISTER: You should wear clothes.
BROTHER: Clothes?
SISTER: In my school, the boys will wear uniforms. They will weara yellow hat, black pants and blue shirts. On their shirts, there will be a bright brass plate with their names. Oh, they are so sweet.

BROTHER: What are you talking about? I don't understand.
SISTER: You should be just like those boys.
BROTHER: Can I keep my diaper if I wear those···clothes?
SISTER: No, you can't.
BROTHER: If I want to pee,what should I do?
SISTER: Well···well···
BROTHER: I don't want to wear clothes.
SISTER: Why?

BROTHER: Diaper is better.

SISTER: That's different.

BROTHER: That's the same.

SISTER: That's different.

BROTHER: That's exactly the same!

SISTER: ⋯I don't understand you. Are you really an idiot?

BROTHER: Who told you that?

SISTER: Everyone.

BROTHER: What about you? Do you think I'm an idiot?

SISTER: I⋯I don't think so.

BROTHER: Then why saying so?

SISTER: When people talking to you, why do you pretend you don't understand them?

BROTHER: I didn't pretend. I really don't understand.

SISTER: Really?

BROTHER: Yes.

SISTER: But you can understand me.

BROTHER: You're talking to me with baby language. It's our language. But those people, they've already forgotten.

SISTER: Really?

BROTHER: Of course.

Silence.

SISTER: Il fait très beau.

BROTHER: What?

SISTER: Tu veux manger quelque chose?

BROTHER: Stop!

SISTER: Tu es un grand benêt.

BROTHER:	Stop that!!!
SISTER:	It's funny!
BROTHER:	No it's not! What did you say just now?
SISTER:	I said, it's a fine day today. Are you hungry? And···You're a fool.
BROTHER:	I'm not a fool.
SISTER:	If you always act like this, nobody will talk to you anymore.
BROTHER:	Why?
SISTER:	Because they don't use our language.
BROTHER:	Because they've abandoned meaningful things and started to get interested in meaningless things. You are also one of them.
SISTER:	What are meaningful things?
BROTHER:	Lying in bed and sucking thumb. Just like me.
SISTER:	Liar.
BROTHER:	If you continue fool around with those guys, you'll be just like them. I'll hate you, too.

Silence.

BROTHER:	Did they take you out somewhere?
SISTER:	Yes.
BROTHER:	You were away for a long time.
SISTER:	Just two weeks.
BROTHER:	Did you have a good time?
SISTER:	Of course. I took ··· avion.
BROTHER:	Avion? What's that?
SISTER:	Avion is a bird, it can fly you to the sky.
BROTHER:	Bird? Just like that noisy thing over there?
SISTER:	No. Avion is not a real bird, it's very big and it is made of iron. It has an empty belly and many

small windows. When you look through those windows, you can see small buildings and small human beings. Just like toys.

BROTHER: That's horrible.

SISTER: Not at all. It's a lot of fun.

BROTHER: What else did you do?

SISTER: We went canoter.

BROTHER: Canoter? What's that?

SISTER: It's just like when you are sleeping in your cradle. Imagine there is water everywhere⋯

Sister starts to shake the cradle.

SISTER: You will float on the water⋯Very quiet. The sun will warm your face.

BROTHER: That's great. I love canoter.

SISTER: Come with us next time.

BROTHER: No.

SISTER: Why?

BROTHER: If I can canoter here, why do I have to go there?

SISTER: You can see many more interesting stuff.

BROTHER: No.I want to stay here, safe and sound.

SISTER: I know, I know. You can stay with your thumb.

BROTHER: You're absolutely right.

SISTER: Don't you want to make acquaintance with other people?

BROTHER: No.

SISTER: Why?

BROTHER: All the people in the world look just like you and me. I can make acquaintance with everyone if I make a good acquaintance with you.

SISTER: They are totally different from you and me.

BROTHER: I know you are lying. You want to cheat me to go there. I won't be fooled.

SISTER: As you wish. I'm hungry. I'll go find something to eat.

BROTHER: Please! If you go away, I will be left alone. You will be left alone too.

SISTER: I'm not alone. I have a lot of friends there.

BROTHER: What about me?

SISTER: You can come with me.

BROTHER: No way!

SISTER: Then nobody will play with you!

BROTHER: I can play with my own thumb.

Sister goes off the stage.

SCENE III

Brother starts to suck his thumb. Lights off.

Lights on. Brother is sitting in bed, watching TV. He is laughing.

TV: Hello my friend! GOOD-MORNING!

BROTHER: Morning!

TV: Are you ready?

BROTHER: Yes I'm ready!

TV: One, two, three, go!

It's a good good day and pink goat wakes up.

BROTHER: It's a good good day and pink goat wakes up.

TV: Everything is boring everything looks the same!

BROTHER: Everything is boring everything looks the same!

TV: Very good. Remember now?

BROTHER: Yes!

TV: One, two, three, go!

Brother starts to sing.

BROTHER: It's a good good day and pink goat wakes up.

Everything is boring everything looks the same!

He is not happy cause no sun in the sky!

He knocks at neighbor's door,

Neighbor sees him and says,

Ah it's you! Stupid pink goat!

Neighbor laughs loud and feels great.

His head is smashed to pieces in a second.

Pink goat knocks and knocks with a gun.

Pink goat kills everybody in the small town.

Oh yeah oh yeah, pink goat is a hero.

Oh yeah oh yeah, pink goat is a hero.

Brother laughs.

Sister enters the stage. She is wearing high school uniform. She sits beside her brother.

SISTER:	Brother.
BROTHER:	Ah you're back.
SISTER:	Yes.
BROTHER:	You went away for a long time.
SISTER:	Am I? Oh···You're watching this again.
BROTHER:	Shh···
SISTER:	How long have you been watching?
BROTHER:	I can't remember. Haha···
SISTER:	Change channels! Now!
BROTHER:	···Leave me alone···Come on, come on···BANG! Yeah!
SISTER:	He blows the pig's brain out! Gross!
BROTHER:	Come, sit on my bed and watch with me.
SISTER:	Silly.

Sister turns off the TV.

BROTHER:	What?
SISTER:	You can't watch this anymore.
BROTHER:	Why?
SISTER:	You can't watch télé for too long.

BROTHER:	Télé?
SISTER:	You can't take your eye of it by the time they bought télé for you.
BROTHER:	Ah, his name is télé.
SISTER:	I told you.
BROTHER:	Télé is great. He can tell me everything happens on the other side.
SISTER:	Hum.
BROTHER:	Some are funny, some are horrible.
SISTER:	Hum.
BROTHER:	I can know everything happens on your side if I watch télé here. Then we can have the same topic. Then you won't feel bored if you stay with me.
SISTER:	Hum.
BROTHER:	Then I don't need to leave here.
SISTER:	I knew it.
BROTHER:	So let me play with télé!

Brother turns on the TV.

BROTHER:	Haha···
SISTER:	Stop it!

Sister turns off the TV with the remote control.

BROTHER:	Give me that.
SISTER:	No.
BROTHER:	Give it to me. Now.
SISTER:	NO.
BROTHER:	I will count from one to three. If you don't give that to me···

SISTER: I do this for you.

BROTHER: One, two··· Two···

SISTER: You will act bad if you continue watching this.

BROTHER: Three.

Brother jumps on sister and bites her hand.

Sister screams.

Brother takes back the remote control and turns on the TV.

BROTHER: Haha···

Sister stands up and unplugs the TV.

BROTHER: You killed télé!

SISTER: Stop watching it.

BROTHER: You broke off the string of télé's belly!

SISTER: What're you talking about?

BROTHER: Ah!!! Télé is dead!

SISTER: Stop crying!

BROTHER: Télé is my best friend. He always talks to me. He's not like you. You always leave me alone. Why did you kill him?

SISTER: He is not dead···Télé can't die!

BROTHER: Give me back my télé! Or I'll fucking blow your brain out!!

(Silence.)

BROTHER: Please···I beg you···

SISTER: Ok, if you stop watching télé, I'll stay with you.

BROTHER: Really?

SISTER: Yes.

BROTHER: You won't go there?

SISTER: No. Never.

BROTHER: Great. Great. I forgive you.

Brother starts to suck his thumb.

SISTER: Brother.

BROTHER: Yes?

SISTER: I came across something strange today on the other side.

BROTHER: What?

SISTER: The executive came to our school today. The teacher asked us girls to queue up. We did exercise for the executive.

BROTHER: And then?

SISTER: The teacher asked us to wear the same uniform. The same shirt, the same skirt, the same white socks.

BROTHER: Hum.

SISTER: I stood on a tall platform to lead everyone.

BROTHER: Really? I didn't know you can do exercise.

SISTER: Of course. I'm the best in my school.

BROTHER: Could you please do it for me?

SISTER: Now?

BROTHER: Please, please, do it for me.

Sister hesitates for a moment. She stands up and starts to do exercise.

SISTER: 1,2,3,4. 2, 2, 3, 4. 3,2,3,4⋯

Brother follows the movements of sister. He can just move the upper part of his body.

SISTER: We were wearing the same uniform. The same shirt, the same skirt, the same white socks.

BROTHER: 4,2,3,4. 5,2,3,4. 6,2,3,4. It's great fun!

SISTER: I looked down from the platform. Everyone was following my movements. I felt proud of myself.

BROTHER: This is great fun! Great fun!

SISTER: I kicked my left leg. Everyone kicked their left legs. I lifted my right hand. Everyone lifted their right hands.

BROTHER: 1,2,3,4. 2, 2, 3, 4. 3,2,3,4···

SISTER: It was hot. I was sweating. Everyone was sweating.

BROTHER: 4,2,3,4. 5,2,3,4. 6,2,3,4··· It's great fun!

SISTER: I turned around. Everyone turned around. Now turn around!

BROTHER: Haha!

SISTER: I jumped and everyone started to jump. Now jump!

BROTHER: WOW!!

SISTER: I could control everyone!

BROTHER: 5,2,34,. 6,2,3,4.

SISTER: I tried harder and harder. I kicked my leg as high as my head!

BROTHER: This is much fun than télé!

SISTER: Left hand!

BROTHER: Left hand!

SISTER: Right hand!

BROTHER: Right hand!

TOGETHER: 1,2,3,4. 2,2,3,4. 3,2,3,4. 4,2,3,4.

They do exercise like crazy.

SISTER: In the end, everyone on the square looks just like me. The same shirt, the same skirt, the same white socks.

BROTHER: 7,2,3,4. 8,2,3,4. And 1,2,3,4. 2,2,3.4. Yeah!

SISTER: I found out that their faces were starting to become as same as mine.

Sister stops. Brother is still doing exercise like crazy.

BROTHER: Why do you stop?

SISTER: I don't want to do it any more.

BROTHER: Why?

SISTER: I wanted to see whether the others will also stop just like me.

BROTHER: Why?

SISTER: They didn't stop. They continued doing exercise.

BROTHER: Why?

SISTER: I don't know. I was scared.

BROTHER: Why! It's great fun! Come and do exercise with me!

Sister finds out that brother cannot stop himself.

SISTER: Stop···stop it. What happened?

BROTHER: 1,2,3,4. 2,2,3,4.

SISTER: Stop.

BROTHER: 3,2,3,4. 4,2,3,4. WOW! This is amazing!

SISTER: Stop!!

Sister slaps him. Brother suddenly stops.

BROTHER:	Oh⋯
SISTER:	I'm sorry.
BROTHER:	What happened just now?
SISTER:	Nothing.
BROTHER:	Oh⋯
SISTER:	What's wrong?
BROTHER:	My face hurts. My arm hurts. My body hurts⋯
SISTER:	I think you are right.
BROTHER:	What?
SISTER:	Everyone on the other side looks just the same as you and me.
BROTHER:	So?
SISTER:	I want to stay here and suck thumb with you.
BROTHER:	Welcome! You just need a little bed to lie down, just like when we were babies.
SISTER:	OK.

Silence.

BROTHER:	Would you please continue?
SISTER:	Continue?
BROTHER:	Continue doing exercise for me.
SISTER:	What do you mean?
BROTHER:	I saw many girls doing exercise on télé, they looked just like you.
SISTER:	So?
BROTHER:	I feel excited when I watch this. I feel so hot. And⋯and something in my diaper will stand up. It's great fun.
SISTER:	⋯
BROTHER:	Oh, you told me that you don't have this thing. So you will never have this kind of feeling.

SISTER:	···
BROTHER:	I love watching you doing exercise. Would you please do it for me? Please!

Sister stands up.

SISTER:	I thought you are a good guy.
BROTHER:	What?
SISTER:	I thought you are still a little boy, lying in bed, sucking thumb and don't understand their language.
BROTHER:	I can sit. You see, I can sit now.
SISTER:	I thought you were innocent!
BROTHER:	What?
SISTER:	You are talking the same thing just as those people!
BROTHER:	I don't understand.
SISTER:	The other side is horrible. Here is also horrible.
BROTHER:	Why you're not happy? Are you hungry?

Brother stretches out his thumb.

BROTHER:	Here you are.
SISTER:	I hate you.
BROTHER:	Why?
SISTER:	I don't want to talk to you anymore.

Sister starts to pack.

BROTHER:	Where are you going? You promised me you will never leave me! Give me back my télé before you go away!

Sister turns on the TV.

SISTER: Fine. Go ahead! MERDE!

Sister goes off the stage. Brother continues watching TV.

BROTHER: Ha.. 1,2,3,4. 2,2,3,4. Oh Yeah blew her brain out!
                3,2,3,4. 4,2,3,4.

Lights off.

SCENE IV

Lights on. Brother is alone on stage. His baby diaper is dirty.
His bed is dirty. Everything is dirty.

Brother makes strange laughs. He rolls on the ground from the
side of the bed.

BROTHER: Oh I'm tired.

Brother puts the quilt on his head.

BROTHER: It stinks!

Brother smells his baby diaper.

BROTHER: It stinks! It stinks!

Brother starts to talk to his thumb.

BROTHER: Hey thumb. She has been away for a long time.
THUMB: Yes.
BROTHER: Can you tell me why?
THUMB: I think she hates you, you asshole.
BROTHER: What should I do to bring her back?
THUMB: She'll never come back. You idiot.
BROTHER: What should I do?
THUMB: You know the answer.
BROTHER: Do I need to leave here to find her?
THUMB: Of course.

BROTHER:	But I can't do anything. Would you please teach me? Hey!

Thumb stops moving. Brother starts to talk to big toe.

BROTHER:	Hey big toe. She has been away for a long time.
TOE:	···Ah?
BROTHER:	Could you tell me why?
TOE:	Oh.
BROTHER:	What should I do to bring her back?
TOE:	Eh.
BROTHER:	Do I need to leave here to find her?
TOE:	Um.
BROTHER:	Um.

Brother tries hard to climb to the right side of the stage.
Sister enters the stage. She is wearing a suit. She pulls
brother back to the bed.

SISTER:	You are such a bad boy. What do you want to do?
BROTHER:	AHAHAH& (@*&%#*——
SISTER:	It stinks··· Would you please sit back? I don't want to worry about you all the time.
BROTHER:	Sit.. Sit..
SISTER:	Yes. SIT.
BROTHER:	AHEHHHHH···..
SISTER:	I don't understand you.
	Listen. I'll go somewhere far away from now on.
BROTHER:	···far away···
SISTER:	Yes, far away. I'm getting married.
BROTHER:	Huh?
SISTER:	MARRIED.

BROTHER:	MARR···
SISTER:	MARRIED. Getting married··· means to be with each other forever.

Brother suddenly holds on to sister.

BROTHER:	MARRIED! MARRIED!
SISTER:	We can't get married because we are brother and sister.
BROTHER:	Ehhhhhh···
SISTER:	I can't take care of you anymore because I'll have to take care of someone else. But don't worry, I've found somewhere better. I'll send you there tomorrow. I'll come to see you.
BROTHER:	···
SISTER:	Anyway, you don't understand a word.

Sister puts brother on bed and goes off the stage.
After a short silence, brother starts to talk to thumb.

BROTHER:	Hey thumb, do you understand what she said?
THUMB:	Of course you stupid asshole.
BROTHER:	She's getting marri..marri..
THUMB:	Married.
BROTHER:	Does it mean she will leave me forever?
THUMB:	You know the answer.
BROTHER:	Did I do something wrong?
THUMB:	Don't ask me! Idiot!
BROTHER:	Don't blame me! She won't like you if she doesn't like me!

Thumb stops moving. Brother starts to talk to big toe.

BROTHER:	Big toe, do you understand what she said?
TOE:	Ah?
BROTHER:	Does it mean she will leave me forever?
TOE:	Eh··· Um.
BROTHER:	Did I do something wrong?

Big toe shakes and makes a negative tone.

BROTHER:	Thank you.

Brother sucks his big toe.
Lights off.

SCENE V

Lights on.

Sister and the young man were standing in front of a window and watching towards the side of the audience. Sister rests her head on young man's chest.

SISTER: Look.

YOUNG MAN: Hum.

SISTER: Are you looking at your baby?

YOUNG MAN: Yes I am.

SISTER: Do you know which one is your baby?

YOUNG MAN: Well···

SISTER: Come on, don't tell me you cannot recognize your own baby!

YOUNG MAN: I see him, darling. I'm now looking at him.

SISTER: Tell me which one is your baby.

YOUNG MAN: The one who is sucking his thumb.

SISTER: That's not our baby!

YOUNG MAN: So··· which one is?

SISTER: The one beside the window who is sleeping!

YOUNG MAN: Oh I see.

SISTER: What a good daddy.

YOUNG MAN: Calm down, I'm now looking at him.

SISTER: Sucking thumb is a bad habit. We should prevent our baby from doing this.

YOUNG MAN: You're the boss.

SISTER: Look, he is so cute.

YOUNG MAN: Yes.

SISTER: It seems that babies will never wake up if they fall asleep.

YOUNG MAN: You know what, it reminds me of my former workplace.

SISTER: What?

YOUNG MAN: Plastic doll factory.

SISTER: ...

YOUNG MAN: All the plastic dolls were made from the same mold so every doll looks just the same.

SISTER: Why are you telling me this?

YOUNG MAN: Just occurs to me. You see, those babies look the same. They are lying in the same bed, wrapped in the same towel. They all have small noses and small eyes. Everyone looks just like my son.

SISTER: You will get to know baby as time goes on. Each person in the world differs from one another.

YOUNG MAN: Really?

SISTER: Even twins are different.

YOUNG MAN: Are you sure?

SISTER: Of course. Come, let's go.

YOUNG MAN: Honey. I want to stay here with our baby for a while. You go first.

SISTER: Ok, don't stay too long.

Sister goes off the stage.

After a short silence, young man starts to talk to his thumb.

YOUNG MAN: Hey thumb, I am a father now. Do you know which one is my baby? You don't know either, do you? Everyone looks just the same. How can I tell myself from others? I will never feel safe until I see someone who looks just like me. It's horrible, isn't it? I wish I could find another ME on the other side as soon as possible. It's not my fault, right?

How I wish I could cry.

Young man puts his thumb in his mouth. Babies start to cry.

Lights off.

SCENE VI

Lights on. Brother sits on a hobbyhorse. The old man sits in a rocking chair.

Brother speaks to the thumb.

BROTHER: Hey, thumb, do you like living here?

THUMB: Well···

BROTHER: Not so bad. I thought other places were horrible. However, it seems like there's no difference between my room and the outside world.

THUMB: You can eat well and sleep well here. That's enough. Asshole.

BROTHER: Yes. But my sister has been away for a long time.

THUMB: You can't understand her language.

BROTHER: Yes. She has changed. She has became just like others.

THUMB: It's all your fault. You should stay with her. But you let her go. You should keep looking for yourself on the other side. It's your mission.

BROTHER: But how?

Thumb stops moving. Brother speaks to his big toe.

BROTHER: Hey, big toe. Do you know that guy beside you?

TOE: Eh?

BROTHER: He has been here for a long time.

TOE: Oh.

BROTHER: I guess he can't understand us either.

TOE: Eh.

BROTHER:	But he also likes sucking his thumb.
TOE:	Mmm..
BROTHER:	Could you say hello to him?
TOE:	Uh-huh.

Brother turns his foot to the old man.

BROTHER:	Hello! You looks just like me. Who are you? Where did you come from? Forget it. He don't understand a word.

Brother begins to suck his thumb.

OLD MAN:	Whooo air you? Where di...d you g···gome f··· from?
BROTHER:	What?
OLD MAN:	Who are you? Where did you··· come from?
BROTHER:	Are you talking to me? Do you understand what I'm saying?
OLD MAN:	Well··· they···they don't understand.
BROTHER:	Oops!
OLD MAN:	What's···what's wrong?
BROTHER:	It's my ear. I'm not accustomed to hearing the same language.
OLD MAN:	I've been···stopped talking like this for···a long time.
BROTHER:	Why?
OLD MAN:	If I talk like this, they will feed me···and change my···my···
BROTHER:	Baby diaper?
OLD MAN:	Yes! Baby diaper! Or they will let me watch··· watch···

Old man points forward.

OLD MAN: Do you know what that is?

BROTHER: That's télé.

OLD MAN: Yes! If I talk like this, they will say: Shut up! And let me watch télé.

BROTHER: They will do the same thing to me. She said because there's something wrong with···my head.

OLD MAN: Who's she?

BROTHER: She and me,we came from the same place.

OLD MAN: Well. So we'd better stop talking like this, and speak their language. Then they will stop bothering us.

BROTHER: You can speak their language?

OLD MAN: Yes.

BROTHER: Did you spend a long time with them?

OLD MAN: Too long for me to remember myself. I find myself again until once I met someone looked the same as me.

BROTHER: Looks the same as you? Really? Where did you meet him?

OLD MAN: I met him when I was a solider.

BROTHER: I know! I once saw soldiers in télé!

OLD MAN: I hid behind a tree. Guns were firing and bullets were flying about everywhere.

BROTHER: It was great fun!

OLD MAN: Suddenly I heard someone shouting: OPEN FIRE! OPEN FIRE! I jumped out but I couldn't move at all.

BROTHER: Why?

OLD MAN: A man was running towards me. He looked the same as me.

BROTHER:	Wow! Us on the other side!
OLD MAN:	I looked around. I found out everyone looked just the same as me. What the hell!
BROTHER:	Us on the other side···
OLD MAN:	It was dreadful. You were coming to kill yourself.
BROTHER:	Dreadful.
OLD MAN:	The man in front was running towards me. What should I do?
BROTHER:	What should you do?
OLD MAN:	Should I kill him or not? Maybe he is my true self. If I kill him, my true self will die at the same time.
BROTHER:	Did you kill him?
OLD MAN:	··· Yes I did.
BROTHER:	What a pity.
OLD MAN:	Not so long ago, I drove through a long tunnel.
BROTHER:	Just like the long pipe?
OLD MAN:	Yes.
BROTHER:	A narrow pipe. A dark pipe. Too dark for me to see the string on my belly.
OLD MAN:	It was midnight. I drove and drove. The tunnel suddenly became so long and there was no ending.
BROTHER:	Oh.
OLD MAN:	Suddenly I vaguely saw a group of people in front of me.
BROTHER:	Who were they?
OLD MAN:	I stopped the car and waited for them. They came closer and closer, I found out that they were wearing military uniforms and looked tired. Everyone was walking slowly without making any sound.
BROTHER:	What did they look like?

OLD MAN: They looked familiar.

BROTHER: Who were they?

OLD MAN: I rolled down the window and shouted to them:
            Hey! Who---Are---You? Where---Did---You---
            Come---From? Where---Are---You---Going?

BROTHER: No one answered you.

OLD MAN: Except the last one. He took a glance at me. I
            suddenly recognized him!

BROTHER: Who was he?

OLD MAN: The man I killed in battle.

BROTHER: The one who looked the same as you?

OLD MAN: Exactly.

BROTHER: So that was YOURSELF.

OLD MAN: I suddenly took pity on him so I shouted at him:
            Hey, do you need a ride?

Silence.

OLD MAN: Then everyone stopped and looked back at me.

BROTHER: And then?

OLD MAN: Everyone looked the same as me.

BROTHER: Great!

OLD MAN: I started my car and drove out of the tunnel.

BROTHER: Why?

OLD MAN: My car is too small to carry so many people.

BROTHER: You are so lucky. You can meet us on the other
            side so frequently.

OLD MAN: They were all the people I killed in battle.

BROTHER: And then?

OLD MAN: And then they sent me here.

BROTHER: How does it feel when you kill someone?

OLD MAN: I can't remember.

BROTHER:	Just like the Pink Goat who killed his neighbors?
OLD MAN:	What?
BROTHER:	Do you have a gun?
OLD MAN:	Yes I once had a gun.
BROTHER:	Are you unhappy if there's no sun in the sky?
OLD MAN:	I guess no one will feel good about that.
BROTHER:	Has anyone once told you that you're stupid?
OLD MAN:	Ah, I was told many times.
BROTHER:	Are you Pink Goat?
OLD MAN:	What's that?
BROTHER:	You're Pink Goat! But you don't know!
OLD MAN:	Maybe. I don't know too much about the world.
BROTHER:	You are a hero!
OLD MAN:	That's exactly what they call me.
BROTHER:	You know what! I have been adoring you since very young age!

Silence.

BROTHER:	Are you wearing baby diaper?
OLD MAN:	Yes.
BROTHER:	Do you have that thing in your diaper?
OLD MAN:	What thing?
BROTHER:	Here. Look.

Brother let the old man look into his diaper.

OLD MAN:	Yes, I do.

Old man let brother look into his diaper.

BROTHER: Great! We came from the same place!

OLD MAN: Great.

Brother looks into the old man's eyes.

BROTHER: I can see myself from your eyes.

OLD MAN: Me too.

They looked into the eyes of each other for a long time.

BROTHER: I look just like you.

OLD MAN: I think so.

BROTHER: We look great.

OLD MAN: Yeah.

BROTHER: I've been always loving myself.

OLD MAN: Me too.

BROTHER: We are the same. I love myself so I should love you.

OLD MAN: Yeah.

BROTHER: So I'm another Pink Goat? So I'm also a hero?

OLD MAN: I guess so.

Brother stretches out his thumb.

BROTHER: Here you are.

OLD MAN: What?

BROTHER: Have a taste of it.

The old man sucked brother's thumb.

BROTHER: Does it have a different flavor?

The old man sucked his thumb.

OLD MAN: They taste the same!

They laughed. The old man started to yawn.

Brother started to yawn. They laughed.

The old man farts. Brother farts. They laughed.

The old man starts to sneeze. Brother starts to sneeze. They laughed.

They start to suck their own thumb. Lights off.

-THE END-

《那邊的我們》

二〇一六年四月二十八日
首演於台北牯嶺街小劇場，
盜火劇團主辦及演出。

編　　劇：劉天涯
導演暨藝術總監：謝東寧
製 作 人：蟻薇玲
舞台暨服裝設計：何睦芸
燈光設計：蘇揚清
音樂設計：許博烝
平面設計：葛昌惠
舞台監督：葉玟嵐
執行製作：黃澄閑
CF導演攝影暨剪輯：楊博達

演　　員：徐浩忠 飾 哥哥
　　　　　湯軒柔 飾 妹妹

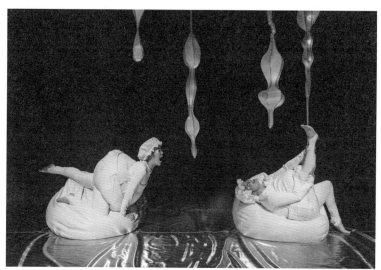

photo credit：陳又維

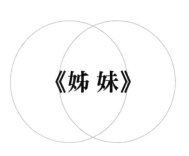

《姉 妹》

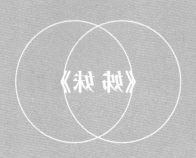

角色

姐姐

妹妹

「我和兩個好友走在小徑上—正是夕陽西下時—突然之間，天空轉為血紅色—我停步，感到精疲力盡，倚靠在欄杆上—血光和火舌，在深藍色的峽灣和城市之上肆虐—我的朋友們繼續向前走著，我站在原地，焦慮地顫抖。

—我感到一聲巨大無窮的吶喊聲劃過天空，響徹蒼穹。」

—愛德華・孟克

第一場

（客廳燈微亮，姐姐坐在客廳的餐桌上。）

（從黑暗中，傳來一個低沉的帶有回音的男聲。）

男人 妳的畫跟妳的家有很大關係，跟我談談妳的家吧。

（姐姐思考片刻。）

姐姐 我家的冬天，很溫暖，樹都還是綠色的，不用穿厚大衣，也沒有鏟雪
車。只有馬路上偶爾駛過的機車，引擎聲非常巨大，就像一聲尖叫劃過
空氣，然後又是一片寂靜…這裡也跟從前一模一樣。什麼都沒有變。又
老又舊的霉味，很熟悉，窗外的那棵芒果樹也還在。我離開的時候就是
這樣，房子就在這裡，什麼都沒變過。
她也是一樣。

（鑰匙聲窸窣，妹妹上場，她面容疲憊，拿著一把傘。手裡還拿著賬單。）

（妹妹收好傘，她開始看賬單。她似乎看不到姐姐。）

姐姐 最起碼第一眼看到她的時候，我是這麼想的。
那個晚上是我們最後一次見面。
當我離開這個房子之後，我們再也沒有見過彼此。

（妹妹輕輕推開臥室的門，微弱的燈光透進，她把門關上。）

姐姐 其實…我很抱歉，雖然我沒有真的跟她這樣講…
後來，當然…我有寫信給她，我告訴她，我的那些畫，堆滿二樓小房間
的那些畫，現在變得很值錢了，如果她有需要的話，她可以……那是我
送給她的，是她的財產。

我不知道自己要怎麼彌補她，這是我能想到唯一的方式——

但她沒有回信。

第二場

（妹妹的聲音從臥室傳來。）

妹妹　（在臥室內）姐，姐——？
姐姐　啊？怎麼了？
妹妹　（開門伸出頭）妳可不可以幫我拿一件小寶的內衣。
姐姐　好啊，在哪裡？
妹妹　在後面的院子里。衣架上面。
姐姐　噢，好。

（姐姐起身，下場。）

姐姐　（場外）這邊有好多件呀，妳要的是哪件？
妹妹　有大象的那件。
姐姐　（場外、自言自語）大象，大象在哪裡…
妹妹　有看到嗎？
姐姐　（場外）我正在找。
妹妹　就是有大象的那一件啊。
姐姐　…
妹妹　沒關係。
姐姐　（場外）什麼？

（妹妹從臥室出，進客廳，穿越舞台，往院子方向出場。）

妹妹　（場外）我說沒關係，我自己來。
姐姐　（場外）噢。

（妹妹拿著一件衣服，經過客廳，穿越舞台，進入臥室。）

（姐姐尾隨妹妹出，她想看臥室裡面，但妹妹隨手把門關上了。）

（片刻之後，妹妹從臥室出來，她小心地關上門，吐了一口氣。）

姐姐 小寶睡啦？

妹妹 嗯，終於。唉，我太忙了，小寶的衣服都是積了一堆才洗。

（姐妹兩人坐在沙發上。）

姐姐 累了吧。

妹妹 還好，這麼大的小孩子就是這樣，醒了就很難睡著的。習慣就好。

姐姐 小寶長得跟妳很像。

妹妹 嗯？

姐姐 小寶啊。特別是鼻子。

妹妹 噢！對啊…但是個性不像。

　　　小寶的個性，有點像妳。

姐姐 是嘛？這麼小就看得出來？

（姐妹笑。）

妹妹 哎，妳看我忙著講話，都忘記開燈了，這麼暗，不好意思。

（妹妹起身去開燈，舞台變得明亮。）

（妹妹在流理台倒水。）

妹妹 要不要喝水？

姐姐 謝謝。

（妹妹開始順手整理房間。）

姐姐 欸，妹，那邊那些大樓，是什麼時候蓋起來的？

妹妹 哪邊？

姐姐 我剛剛在院子看到的，靠山的那邊啊。

妹妹 噢，那就是這幾年啊，從車站那邊，一點一點蓋過來的。

姐姐 車站？

妹妹 對啊，（妹妹起身）來，妳看，（妹妹和姐姐從窗戶看出去）在那裡，看得到嗎？

姐姐 啊，有，我看到了。

哎，妳還記得嗎，我們小時候，這裡整片都是稻田，車站就在那邊，一眼就看得到，好大好大的一棟。真沒想到，現在看起來變這麼小。

妹妹 是啊，那時候一到夏天，很多青蛙叫個不停，吵得人睡不好覺。

姐姐 其實還蠻懷念的。

妹妹 嗯？

姐姐 青蛙啊。

妹妹 噢！嗯，是啊。青蛙。

姐姐 剛剛我還看到山上有很多燈光，是什麼啊？記得從前都沒有。

妹妹 那邊新開了很多家溫泉旅館，現在剛好是旺季，生意很好。

姐姐 噢。

妹妹 有很多旅行團，白天的時候，巴士就一輛一輛的往上面開。

姐姐 老家的變化真大，都快認不出來了。

妹妹 因為妳太久沒回來了。

姐姐 沒辦法啊，我是真的太忙。

妹妹 都快十年啦。

姐姐 我要畫畫啊，要顧展覽，常常是一個電話來，就得收行李準備飛了。

妹妹 …

姐姐 再說，我叫妳過去，妳也不來啊。

妹妹 機票這麼貴，我怎麼能說去就去。

姐姐 我不是說妳可以…

妹妹 再說，我也很忙啊。白天要上班，晚上有時候還得打工…之前，還要照顧爸…後來，有了小孩，更是沒時間。

姐姐 …

妹妹 妳不在，這個家總要有人顧嘛。

姐姐 …

妹妹 對了，今天小寶有沒有乖？

姐姐 有啊，她很乖。我跟她玩了一個下午，她喜歡跟我玩，一直對我笑…

妹妹 那就好。

姐姐 啊，不過，我幫她換尿布的時候，真的有點手忙腳亂，她那麼軟，我不知道該怎麼放她…害她哭個不停…

妹妹 小孩子換尿布都會哭啦。

姐姐 希望我沒有弄痛她…

妹妹 姐，真是不好意思，麻煩妳了。

姐姐 嗯？噢，沒事啊，應該的。

妹妹 我今天實在脫不開身，鄰居阿姨也不在家…

姐姐 欸——

妹妹 嗯？

姐姐 都說沒關係了。這點小事還跟我客氣。

妹妹 …

姐姐 而且，我蠻喜歡小孩的啊。

妹妹 妳？（笑）

姐姐 我知道我從前是完全不會啦，但現在，有時候偶爾會想，如果自己有一個小孩的話，不知道會怎麼樣。

妹妹 妳啊？（笑）妳能把自己照顧好就不錯了。換尿布啊、餵奶啊，都是些生活瑣事，要妳天天做，肯定受不了。

姐姐 …

妹妹 對了，家裡有麻糬，要不要來一點？

姐姐 不用了。

妹妹 可是姐妳不是最喜歡麻糬嗎？

姐姐 真的不用啦。

妹妹 這是知道妳要回來，我特地去買的。（妹妹拿來一盒麻糬給姐姐）妳看。妳知道的嘛，我不吃這個。小時候我一吃麻糬，就拉肚子，害得我一直不敢吃。

姐姐 …

妹妹 吃一點吧，國外應該沒得買。

姐姐 嗯。

（姐姐坐在餐桌前，盯著麻糬看。妹妹倒水。）

妹妹 …怎麼不吃？

姐姐 噢，沒有啊，我在弄。（姐姐把麻糬打開，妹妹端著一杯水，坐在姐姐旁邊。姐姐吃麻糬，露出滿意的表情）嗯——這個味道真的是——欸，妳還記得嗎，上國中的時候，週末都會有一個騎腳踏車，賣麻糬的阿伯，記得嗎？那時候他一來，妳就跟著他車子後面跑，跑著跑著就會跌倒，妳記得嗎？

妹妹 嗯？怎麼了嗎？

姐姐 …噢，沒什麼。這個，很好吃。

妹妹 那就好。

姐姐 吃到這個，才有回家的感覺。

妹妹 我就說嘛。

第三場

妹妹 姐，其實我記得啦。

姐姐 嗯？

妹妹 那個賣麻糬的阿伯。

姐姐 嗯——！

妹妹 他腳踏車後座的木箱裡，就放著一整塊沒切的麻糬。他還會在巷口喊
「麻糬喔—麻糬喔—」那個聲音，我怎麼也忘不了。

姐姐 是啊。

妹妹 我記得那時候，爸爸常常買麻糬給妳。爸爸知道妳喜歡吃。

姐姐 爸爸很疼我們。

妹妹 什麼很疼我們，是很疼妳好不好。鋼琴啊，芭蕾啊，英文家教⋯妳想要
的，爸爸都給妳啊。妳記不記得，有天晚上回來，妳還跟我炫耀鋼琴比
賽的獎牌，還說爸親自開警車，帶妳出門兜風⋯欸，老實說，那時候我
真的很羨慕。

姐姐 都是小時候的事啦。

妹妹 妳還記不記得，那時候爸買太多麻糬了，妳吃不完，都會逼我吃。

姐姐 有嗎？

妹妹 有啊，那時候妳就坐在我的床邊，叫我吃。我不吃，妳就一口一口餵我
吃啊。妳記不記得有時候妳連花生粉都懶得蘸，一大塊直接塞進來，妳
忘了嗎？

（妹妹把姐姐手裡的麻糬塞到姐姐嘴裡，二人笑。）

姐姐 我哪有？

妹妹 有啊，妳那時候還說，我是妳的妹妹，要幫妳分擔。我和妳是一樣的，
都是爸爸的女兒，爸爸的愛心，我們就要一起分享。

姐姐 嗯⋯

妹妹 妳還記不記得，逼我吃麻糬的事，妳不許我告訴爸爸，妳還說，要是我不吃的話，我會被趕出這個家，就跟媽一樣。

姐姐 ⋯我說過嗎？

妹妹 說過。

姐姐 我有點不記得了。

（沉默片刻。）

妹妹 姐，妳有沒有想過，媽媽離開的時候，為什麼不帶走我們？

姐姐 因為法院把撫養權判給爸了啊。

妹妹 是這樣沒錯，可是我們是姐妹啊，姐妹的話，不是應該一人帶走一個，這樣比較公平？

姐姐 我是沒想過。

（沉默片刻。）

妹妹 其實那個時候，媽媽有想帶我走。

姐姐 沒有，她說她想自己一個人走。

妹妹 她有。

姐姐 不可能，妳記錯了。

妹妹 妳不會知道。因為她是偷偷跑來學校問我。她說她不想回家，不想看見爸。

姐姐 可是妳留下來了啊，是妳自己選擇的。

妹妹 不是我啊，是妳。

姐姐 ⋯我？

妹妹 是妳讓我留下的啊，妳不記得了嗎？妳那時候跟我說，媽媽不會回來了，因為她會有一個新的家，會有別的小孩，妳還說需要我陪妳。妳就一直哭一直哭，妳不記得嗎？

姐姐 我說過嗎？

妹妹 有啊。結果我留下了，但妳沒多久就走了，一走就是十年，留下我一個人，跟爸在一起。

姐姐 …

妹妹 姐，我有時候在想，如果當年我跟媽走，是不是事情會變得比較好一點。

姐姐 也有可能比現在更糟啊，這誰知道。

妹妹 也是啦。

第四場

妹妹 姐妳會不會累？

姐姐 不會不會。

妹妹 有點晚了…如果妳要休息的話…

姐姐 （起身去拿外套）沒關係，不用麻煩，真的，再說，旅館我也住習慣了。

妹妹 妳要去旅館？

姐姐 對啊。

妹妹 姐妳回家幹嘛還訂旅館，就住家裡啊。妳的房間我都幫妳整理好了。

姐姐 房間？我的房間？

妹妹 對啊，樓上的房間啊。

姐姐 …妳還幫我留著？

妹妹 當然啊。我帶妳來看。

（妹妹帶著姐姐走上二樓階梯。）

妹妹 妳看，窗簾還是原來那條，家具的位置，桌子上的東西，和妳離開家的
時候一模一樣，除了打掃之外，我平時都不會進去。

姐姐 …噢，沒關係啦，反正我現在躺在床上也睡不著，一定是睜著眼睛到天
亮。

（沉默片刻。）

妹妹 姐，所以妳到現在都沒有好一點嗎？

姐姐 嗯？

妹妹 妳之前…聽起來滿嚴重的。

姐姐 什麼啊？

妹妹 就，妳上次不是晚上睡不著，結果鬧到警察局。

姐姐 喔，不是啦。

妹妹 不是？

姐姐 我現在睡不著是因為時差。

妹妹 啊！對。時差，妳看我，真是的。

姐姐 不是因為那個啦。

妹妹 （很快地）我不是那個意思。

姐姐 （很快地）沒關係。

妹妹 …妳這次回來，飛了多久？

姐姐 快二十個小時吧。

妹妹 這麼久啊。

姐姐 是啊。

　　　之前，我是真的沒辦法睡。

妹妹 …完全都睡不著嗎？

姐姐 對啊，飛機上真的很難睡。

妹妹 噢，妳說飛機。

姐姐 坐長途飛機的時候，時間是完全錯亂的，分不清到底是凌晨還是中午。
　　　人好像在另外一個世界。

妹妹 噢。

姐姐 不過這次不一樣，這次在飛機上，完全挺不住。睡到天昏地暗，連吃了
　　　幾餐都忘記了。好像把之前沒睡夠的，一口氣都補回來了。

妹妹 那太好了。有睡飽就好。

姐姐 …我有跟妳說過嗎？

妹妹 什麼？

姐姐 睡不著的事。

妹妹 嗯，說過。

姐姐 什麼時候？

妹妹 妳半夜打來那次啊。

姐姐 半夜？

妹妹 是啊，我來不及穿衣服就跑去接。

姐姐 我怎麼不記得了。

妹妹 不記得？…妳還哭呢。

姐姐 （笑）我？

妹妹 是啊，妳跟我說妳在警察局，害我嚇了一大跳，以為妳出什麼事了。

姐姐 （笑）妳確定那是我嗎？

妹妹 當然啊。

姐姐 搞不好是妳在做夢啊。

妹妹 是不是做夢這種事，我還是能分清楚的好不好。妳這個人真的很奇怪。

姐姐 …喂，我開玩笑的啦。別生氣嘛。

妹妹 …

姐姐 因為我是真的一點印象也沒有。

妹妹 我知道妳睡不著是真的很難過，但妳有去看醫生嗎？

姐姐 有啊，但，完全找不到理由。

妹妹 是嗎？

姐姐 …有可能是被叫聲吵到了。

妹妹 什麼？

姐姐 …妳有沒有聽說過愛德華·孟克？

妹妹 誰？

姐姐 一個挪威的畫家，他畫過一張畫，一個人在橋上尖叫，那副畫很有名啊。

妹妹 噢，很有名，那…電視一定有播。

姐姐 啊，對，不過那次電視是播，那張畫在紐約被拍賣。

妹妹 賣多少錢啊？

姐姐 如果我沒記錯的話，將近一億兩千萬美金。

妹妹 這麼貴！？

姐姐 我在奧斯陸的美術館有看過真跡，那副畫就在我眼前，好像一伸手就可以摸到一億兩千萬美金。

妹妹 …

姐姐 妳知道嗎，那是一幅很奇怪的畫，畫裡的天空是紅色的，好像火山爆發一樣。

妹妹 紅色的天空？我知道，跟妳的畫很像啊。

姐姐 嗯？

妹妹 妳之前寄給我的那幅，有白色框的，記得嗎？

姐姐 …妳這麼一說，好像是有點像。但其實…不太一樣。

妹妹 噢。

姐姐 …不知道為什麼，我看到那幅畫的時候，那個在橋上尖叫的人，我就想啊，原來他跟我是一樣的。

妹妹 …

姐姐 聽說孟克也常常失眠，他一定也是被尖叫聲吵到睡不著的。

妹妹 什麼意思？

姐姐 妳知道嗎，有一天晚上，我剛要睡，突然就聽到尖叫聲，分貝很高，很尖的那種。

妹妹 哪裡來的啊？

姐姐 我不知道，聲音是從二樓傳來的，我平時畫畫的地方。

妹妹 是什麼樣的叫聲？

姐姐 是人在叫。是一個小女孩的聲音，在叫救命——

妹妹 是誰？

姐姐 我不知道，我到二樓去看，畫室空空的，一個人也沒有。

妹妹 …

姐姐 她每天晚上都會叫，結果到後來，我實在受不了了，我就乾脆開窗跟她一起叫。結果鄰居報警，警察就來把我帶走，我待在醫院兩個星期。

妹妹 那，有查出是什麼原因嗎？

姐姐 沒有，因為她沒有停下來，她還是繼續叫。

後來我就再也不管她了，我就讓她一個人留在樓上。

妹妹 所以…

第五場

姐姐 哎呀，不要老是講我的事了。說說妳吧。

妹妹 我？我沒什麼好說的啦。

姐姐 怎麼會…現在的工作，怎麼樣？

妹妹 就還是老樣子。

姐姐 不是很忙嗎？

妹妹 其實還好，只要站櫃檯。一開始比較難，常常結錯錢，就要從當天的薪水裡扣，上手以後就好了。有時候也會去便利商店打工。

姐姐 也是站櫃檯？

妹妹 什麼都做。

姐姐 噢。

妹妹 可是在便利商店不知道為什麼，常常遇到奇怪的客人啊，奇怪的事什麼的。

姐姐 是怎樣奇怪？

妹妹 …有一次我結賬的時候，有一個客人拿了一條櫻花蝦壽司卷，條碼怎麼都刷不出來，我就改敲編碼，可是也沒用，不曉得為什麼，可能是新上架的貨品，可能是那個條碼有問題，也可能是系統失靈。我就問那個客人，能不能拿另外一個給我刷，他說，沒辦法，這是架上最後一個了。怎麼辦呢，我又不能叫他換別的吃。我往後面看，不知道為什麼，他後面突然間排了好多人，通常櫃檯都會有兩個人，但那天不知道為什麼，我的同事偏偏不在，只有我一個。他後面有兩個上班族，看起來很趕時間，我就馬上重新開系統，隊已經排到最後面的冰箱那裡了，而且已經轉彎了。同事的電話一直打不通，我想打給店長，又想到他今天休假，這時候吵他明天一定會被罵，說不定還會被扣薪水。後面排隊的人已經開始吵起來了，一直在問櫃檯那邊是怎麼回事。那兩個上班族眉頭皺在一起，不停地拿手機看時間，嘴巴就發出那種嘖嘖的聲音，可是那個客人一動不動，一副我今天就非要吃這個櫻花蝦壽司不可的架勢。而且不知道為什麼，…我覺得那個人，他長得有點像爸，我就想，這下完蛋了。

我第一次覺得自己真的很沒用，我這人真的很衰，做什麼都失敗。

然後我就哭了。我就一直說 不好意思，不好意思，對不起，對不起。真的很不好意思！

姐姐 …然後呢？

妹妹 …然後，我不太記得了，那天實在是哭太兇。

後來客人都走了，同事也回來了，店裡沒什麼人，好像什麼也沒發生過。我就拿起他丟在櫃檯上的那個櫻花蝦壽司。

嗶，一下就刷到了。

我取消，再重刷，嗶。又過了。我試了好多次，都是一下就刷到了。

所以剛剛到底是發生什麼事情啊？真是不懂。奇怪！

姐姐 …

妹妹 妳有在聽嗎？

姐姐 有啊，我有在聽啊。

妹妹 妳是不是覺得，這種小事沒什麼好講的。

姐姐 沒有啊，我只是…

妹妹 就說我沒什麼好講的嘛。

姐姐 我只是在想，妳不喜歡做就不要做了。

妹妹 我沒辦法啊，我跟妳不一樣，我沒什麼好選擇的。

姐姐 …

妹妹 可是我喜歡超市，超市不一樣。

姐姐 不都是站櫃檯嗎？

妹妹 不一樣。超市上下班很準時。掃碼聲比較好聽，聲音比較低，嗶—嗶—可以不緊不慢地工作，不用分心做其他事。我就不會緊張。有時候，客人買了很多東西，拉出一條長長的購物單，也很有成就感啊。超市也有很多同事，有問題的話轉過身，整整一排的同事，隨時都問得到。對了，超市還常常做活動，去年聖誕節，我們收銀員每個人都戴了一頂鹿角帽子，我的臉小，戴起來很合適，蠻可愛的。

…我自己覺得啦。

超市比較單純。我這個人，喜歡單純一點。

(沉默片刻。)

妹妹 不過最近超市生意不太好。

姐姐 為什麼？

妹妹 附近新開了一家大型購物中心，就在車站旁邊，什麼都有，連家具都買得到。

姐姐 啊，我昨天坐車經過的時候，有看到。

妹妹 大家都去那邊買，這邊就會倒。同事們都在等那邊的徵人消息，一有機會就會換過去。去外商公司工作，比較辛苦一點，但聽說福利比較好。待在這邊，搞不好明天就失業了。

姐姐 那他呢？他有來看過妳嗎？

妹妹 誰？

姐姐 …

妹妹 噢，他啊。

有啊，兩個月前，來過一次。

姐姐 來要錢嗎？

妹妹 不是啦。

姐姐 他現在有在工作嗎？

妹妹 應該有吧，我不知道，我沒有問。

姐姐 妳這樣不行。

妹妹 我沒問題的。

姐姐 他有責任。

妹妹 …

姐姐 那個時候，妳就應該聽我的。

妹妹 …

姐姐 這個小孩根本就不該出生。

妹妹 姐，我覺得妳沒權力這麼說。

她就是要來，就是要出生，妳沒有權力替她決定。我覺得，妳也沒有權力評論我的生活。任何人都沒有。

姐姐 …我真的搞不懂妳。

妹妹 連我自己也搞不懂我自己啦。

姐，我覺得很奇怪，小孩出生之後，平時消失的那些人都出現了，每個人都想來發表一點意見，我的生活一下變得很熱鬧了。所有人都是一樣，一邊抱著我的寶寶，一邊跟我說，她不該出生。所有人也都跟我說同樣的話 他有責任。

奇怪啊，她是我的小孩。跟他沒什麼關係，跟別人也沒什麼關係。她就是我一個人生出來的小孩。小孩子沒有爸爸，一樣可以過得很好。說不定會過得更好。

我這個人喜歡單純一點，就這樣。

第六場

妹妹 很晚了，妳要不要去休息了。

姐姐 噢，好。

妹妹 我去拿毛巾給妳。

（妹妹上樓，再下樓的時候，手裡拿著毛巾。）

姐姐 （視線開始在房間搜尋）對了，妹，我寄過來的畫…妳都放在哪裡啊？

妹妹 噢！畫啊，我都放在二樓。裡面都是妳的畫，都快堆不下了。

姐姐 二樓啊。

妹妹 我不知道應該掛在哪裡啦，我不懂畫。

姐姐 …

妹妹 姐，其實以後妳也不用特別寄畫給我了，郵費應該也很貴。

姐姐 沒關係啊…再說，除了這個，我也沒什麼別的東西可以送妳了。

（沉默片刻。）

姐姐 所以，妳覺得怎麼樣？

妹妹 什麼？

姐姐 我的畫啊。

妹妹 唉呀，我不懂的。妳趕緊去洗澡啦。

姐姐 隨便說說嘛。

妹妹 我不是專家啦，不敢發表意見。

姐姐 我早就受夠那些所謂專業人士的長篇大論了，藝評人啊收藏家啊專家教授，各種術語繞來繞去，還不是在原地打轉。

妹妹 …

姐姐 妳隨便說說啊，我想聽，什麼都好。

（沉默片刻。）

妹妹　真的要我講噢？

姐姐　嗯。

妹妹　怎麼說呢…姐，妳還記不記得妳國中的時候，每年都拿全校美術比賽的
　　　金獎。

姐姐　噢，那是小時候的事了。

妹妹　我很喜歡妳那時候的畫。妳還記得嗎，下雨的港口，很多漁船的那一
　　　幅。

姐姐　噢，記得呀。

妹妹　看的時候，感覺好像真的會有雨水從畫布上流下來一樣。我覺得很厲
　　　害。

姐姐　是嗎。

妹妹　風景啊，人啊什麼的，那個時候妳都畫這樣的畫。

姐姐　對，那時候我也畫了很多田。

妹妹　我是真的很喜歡。

姐姐　嗯。

妹妹　…可是自從妳出國以後，我一直不懂。
　　　妳寄給我的每一幅畫，幾乎都是…都是一模一樣的。同樣的一棟郊區房
　　　子，同樣一扇打開的窗戶，同樣的一個男人，坐在餐桌前面。

姐姐　…

妹妹　到底是怎麼回事？妳從前不是這樣子的。是不是我哪裡搞錯了，還
　　　是…？

姐姐　…

妹妹　唉，就說我不懂畫嘛。

姐姐　妹，其實妳說的沒錯…從出國到現在，我的確都在畫同樣的東西。

妹妹　妳是說…一樣的東西，妳畫了十年？

姐姐　嗯。

妹妹　…

姐姐 我試過很多次，站在空白的畫布前，深呼吸，告訴自己：好！從現在開始，來點別的什麼吧…什麼都好…但一點用也沒有。無論我眼睛睜開還是閉上，無論怎麼畫，我的腦海裡總是會自動出現那棟房子，那個場景…

妹妹 …

姐姐 好像是某個開關被打開。我自己也不知道到底怎麼了。

其他的東西，也不是不能畫，但常常畫了一半，就停了。

可是去年，我的畫有在紐約的一家私人畫廊展出。展我畫的房子系列，一共展了十二張。

我記得那天在下雨，有個小男孩跟他的媽媽來畫廊裡躲雨。一個很可愛的小男孩，他進來繞了一圈，然後站在角落，盯著我的畫。我突然很想問他的意見，所以我就走過去，蹲下來問他：「你看到了什麼？」

然後他就指著畫上的那個男人，問我說：「這個人是誰？」

我說，「這是爸爸」。

然後，他突然回過頭，他問我說，「其他人呢？如果爸爸在這裡，其他人呢？其他人在房子的哪裡呢？」

他這樣問我。

妹妹 妳現在跟我說這個幹什麼？

（沉默片刻。）

姐姐 其實，我這次回來，是有事想跟妳商量。

妹妹 什麼事？

姐姐 爸的遺產。

妹妹 遺產？妳出國之前，我們不是已經達成協議了嗎？妳忘了？

姐姐 我知道，可是…

妹妹 爸留下的本來就不多啊，兩本存摺裡的現金，加上套現的股票，平均分成兩份，一份給妳，一份給我。

姐姐 這個我知道。

妹妹 所以有什麼問題嗎？

姐姐 …我說的是這裡。這棟房子。

妹妹 …

姐姐 如果我沒記錯,房子應該是登記在我和妳的名下吧。

妹妹 對啊,所以?

姐姐 我只是在想,這房子這麼大,妳一個人住,難免也會有孤單的時候吧…

妹妹 妳的意思是——

(姐姐點點頭。妹妹起身,坐到沙發上。)

妹妹 姐,妳真的很自私。

姐姐 不是,妹,妳聽我說…我知道妳喜歡這裡,我知道對妳來說,世界上沒
有任何一個地方比這裡更好了,但我跟妳不一樣——

妹妹 對,妳說的沒錯,我們不一樣。我們是真的不一樣。
妳在國外跑展覽,飛來飛去,倫敦,巴黎,東京,舊金山…到那些我連
想都沒想過的地方去。我呢,大概這輩子就只能呆在這個鄉下小地方,
呆在這房子裡。

姐姐 我不是這個意思。

妹妹 這麼久以來,爸也都是我一個人在照顧。在醫院的時候,他每天都問
我,「姐姐呢,姐姐什麼時候要回來?」我都不知道怎麼回答他。他走
的時候,妳人都不知道在哪。爸的後事,也都是我一個人處理。
現在妳回來了,一見面,就要跟我分家產嗎?

姐姐 妳誤會我了…

妹妹 姐,妳看妳,妳從小到大就是這樣,想做什麼就做什麼,替別人做決
定,所有人都要聽妳的…妳憑什麼啊?

姐姐 …

妹妹 賣房子的事,妳想都別想。

(妹妹提起姐姐的行李箱,走上二樓。)

(姐姐一個人留在客廳。)

(片刻之後,妹妹下樓。)

妹妹 剛剛的一切,就當做沒有發生過。從今往後,我們跟以前一樣,各過各的。妳明天幾點的飛機?

姐姐 可是我不想再畫了。

妹妹 什麼?

姐姐 房子,我畫夠了。

妹妹 到底什麼意思?

(妹妹進臥室。)

姐姐 房子,一共三層,頂樓是挑高的天花板,鑲嵌著木頭裝飾,一樓的客廳,有魚缸和水晶吊燈,一年到頭,窗子永遠開著。每次我從學校宿舍回家,都會遠遠地從窗戶看到夜燈透出來的光,我就知道爸還沒睡,他還在等我。

那天,我像往常一樣回家,推開二樓的房門,四周靜悄悄的,只有魚缸的過濾器發出很細很小的流水聲,然後,我看到爸爸披著他的外套,坐在門口。他說,「妳,站住。過來。」

妳知道的,他一直都是這樣啊。從小他就教我們要乖乖聽話,他說的每一個字,我們都必須照做,沒有人敢違抗他。講話永遠是很冷、很短,像在發號施令。爸做一輩子警察嘛,妳也看過啊,他是怎麼教訓下面的人的。

(妹妹從臥室出來。)

妹妹 妳可以小聲一點嗎?我很累,我想休息了。

(妹妹把燈關掉,客廳重新變得昏暗。妹妹躺在沙發上。)

姐姐 我不敢說不,我走過去,坐在他旁邊。我聞到他身上有很濃的酒味。他跟我說 「躺下。」我一動也不敢動,只能看到他肩膀上那顆黃色的小星星…其實我有點緊張,因為我的功課還沒有寫完…然後那顆星星突然就開始晃起來，我覺得有點痛，我很害怕，我想尖叫，我想叫救命，可是他說「閉嘴，妳如果叫的話，我就讓妳從這個家永遠消失，就跟妳媽一樣。」

妹妹 …

姐姐 第二天，我就看到餐桌上放著一包麻糬，是爸買給我的。

妳知道嗎，那天，那個小男孩問我，「其他人呢？房間裡的其他人在哪裡？」是啊，我為什麼沒想過，在那個時候，整個世界好像沒有人存在了，只剩下我跟他兩個人。妳們呢？妳們在這房子的哪裡？

那天，我回到工作室，看到房間裡大大小小滿滿的都是畫，所有的空間，都被這棟房子、這扇窗戶、還有那個男人塞滿了，我突然覺得好累，我不想再畫了。

妹妹 …

姐姐 那時候，我能想到唯一的方法，就是把房子賣掉，我可以什麼都不要，我只是不想跟這棟房子再有任何聯繫，我想把全部的記憶清空，一切重新開始。

這樣妳聽得懂嗎？

第七場

（妹妹從沙發上坐起身，打開燈。她走到餐桌前，開始大口吃麻糬。）

妹妹 其實那時候，他也有買給我啊。

姐姐 ⋯什麼？

妹妹 麻糬啊，麻糬是爸爸的獎勵。爸爸會買麻糬給聽話的乖小孩。

姐姐 欸——

妹妹 但我吃不下。不知道為什麼，我就是吃不下。

姐姐 ⋯妳說⋯妳說他也有買給妳？

妹妹 姐，妳是怎麼做到的？

姐姐 欸—妳有聽到嗎？

妹妹 什麼？

姐姐 小寶哭了。

妹妹 有嗎？沒有啊。我什麼也沒有聽到。
我在問妳，妳是怎麼做到的？

姐姐 可是⋯妹，那個時候⋯妳為什麼不告訴我？

妹妹 有什麼用？

姐姐 我們⋯我們可以去報警啊，我們可以⋯

妹妹 爸是警官，你覺得他們會相信妳，還是相信爸？

姐姐 總有辦法吧，我們是姐妹啊，我們是兩個人，我們總有辦法⋯

妹妹 那妳呢？妳為什麼不說？

姐姐 我⋯

妹妹 算了啦。妳是不會報警的。
有這個把柄，妳就可以更加有恃無恐，對吧？

姐姐 妳在說什麼啊⋯？

妹妹 妳可以想做什麼就做什麼，把一切當做是理所當然。至於我呢？妳根
本不會想到我的感受，因為妳根本打從心裡就覺得爸爸⋯他是不會看上
我的⋯我說的沒錯吧？

姐姐 …

妹妹 爸真的很疼妳，爸捨不得妳走的。

姐姐 不要說了…

妹妹 妳離開之前…用這件事威脅過他吧。爸都跟我說了，他說，如果那時候他不放妳走，妳就——

姐姐 …

妹妹 姐姐，我沒有妳那麼聰明。

姐姐 …

妹妹 過了這麼久才明白，原來我一直以來，都是別人的替代品。

姐姐 他對我好，我很難過，但是…我真的沒有辦法。

妹妹 算了，都過去了。

姐姐 妹，我是真的不知道…

妹妹 沒關係，就當做什麼也沒發生過吧。

第八場

姐姐 那妳呢？妳是怎麼做到的？

妹妹 什麼？

姐姐 …忘記。妳是怎麼忘記的？

妹妹 我什麼也沒做。我做的唯一一件事就是等。

姐姐 等？

妹妹 我等他慢慢變老，等他突然昏倒在家裡不省人事的那一天，等他躺在床上連屎都沒辦法自己擦的時候…我等他求我，我等他說：妹妹，拜託妳啦…拜託…這一天總會來的。我什麼也沒做，我就是等。

姐姐 …

妹妹 他走了，房子就是我一個人的了，這是我和小寶的房子，沒有我的允許，誰也不準進來。平常下班，我哪裡都不想去，我就只想回家。
　　至於他，其實妳說的沒錯，幾個月前，他的確是來要錢的。但我不在意，只要他離小寶遠一點，要多少錢都可以。我真的不在意。但他絕對不能踏進這裡一步。

姐姐 妹，這房子真的太老了，而且這邊房價一定是越來越貴了啊，妳就沒有考慮過…

妹妹 姐！

第九場

姐姐 第二天，我就收拾行李，飛回了紐約。我沒有跟她告別。

兩年之後，倫敦美術館展出了我的房子系列畫作，一共四十六幅，那是我有生以來最大的一次個展。展覽很成功，有一篇畫評，是這樣寫的「⋯扭曲的重複性，單色的線條所營造的焦慮感，幾乎超越了愛德華·孟克，反射出當代人被存在所侵襲的失衡。」

真的是這樣嗎？我不知道⋯

現在，大家只記得孟克那一幅畫的標價，一億兩千萬美元，但沒有人記得，孟克為什麼會畫出那樣的吶喊呢？

我開始接到很多電話，卡車從我家把那些畫載走，畫中二樓的那個小女孩，繼續到世界各地，發出沒有人聽得見的尖叫。收藏家們一邊搶著我的作品，一邊問我，妳什麼時候再出新畫呢？

可是尖叫聲消失了。

房子，我再也沒辦法畫了。

（妹妹走回臥室。）

第十場

（姐姐隔著臥室的門，跟妹妹講話。）

姐姐 太晚了，我該走了。

妹妹 （場外）嗯…

姐姐 睡得這麼香啊。

妹妹 （場外）是啊。

姐姐 好可愛…（輕聲）拜拜，小寶，拜拜。

妹妹 （場外）…妳明天還會來嗎？

姐姐 哦會啊，妳明天幾點下班？

妹妹 （場外）明天我夜班，到很晚。

姐姐 那…需要我幫你帶小寶嗎？

妹妹 （場外）不用了。

姐姐 真的不用？

妹妹 （場外）真的…

姐姐 …那，我走了。

妹妹 （場外）…

姐姐 晚安。

（燈急暗。）

―劇終―

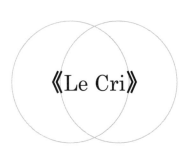

《Le Cri》

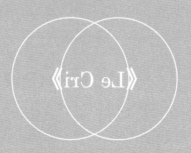

✳THE CHARACTERS:

Elder Sister

Younger Sister

⋯ I was walking along a path with two friends — the sun was setting — suddenly the sky turned blood red — I paused, feeling exhausted, and leaned on the fence — there was blood and tongues of fire above the blue-black fjord and the city — my friends walked on, and I stood there trembling with anxiety — and I sensed an infinite scream passing through nature.

-- Edvard Munch

SCENE I

Dim Lights on, Elder Sister is sitting on the living room table.

A low male voice echoes in the darkness.

THE VOICE: Your paintings is strong related to your hometown. Please tell me something about it.

Elder Sister thinks for a while.

ELDER SISTER: The winter in my hometown is much warmer. The trees were green. You didn't need to wear thick coat and you couldn't see any snowplows down the street. You could only hear the sound of motorbikes···those big sounds of engine, just like a scream passing through the air, then everything comes back to silence···

Everything is the same, nothing changed. The smell of old furniture and the musty room···so familiar to me. The mango tree is still there, standing out of the window. The house looks just exactly the same, nothing ever changed.

(Pause)

Neither does her.

Keys clinking. Enter Younger Sister. She looks quite tired. She is holding an umbrella, with several bills in another hand.

Younger Sister starts to check the bills. It seems that she cannot see Elder Sister.

ELDER SISTER: She hasn't changed···at least I thought so by the first time I saw her···

That was the last night we saw each other.

Since then, we've never met each other again in our whole life.

Younger Sister gently opens the bedroom door.

She enters the room and closes the door.

ELDER SISTER: I feel sorry, actually. Even though I didn't tell her.

Later, of course, I wrote letters. I told her about my paintings. Those paintings piling up the attic, the small room on the second floor. I told her that they've became quite valuable. She could do anything to them···if she wanted. I gave them to her. They were her property.

I don't know how to make it up. This is the only way I could think of.

(Pause)

But she never replied.

SCENE II

The voice of Younger Sister comes through the bedroom.

THE VOICE OF YOUNGER SISTER:

Sister. Sister—?

ELDER SISTER: Yes?

Younger Sister opens the door and keep it half-opened.

YOUNGER SISTER: Could you please fetch me the baby pajama?

ELDER SISTER: Sure. Where did you put them?

YOUNGER SISTER: In the backyard, on the hanger.

ELDER SISTER: Oh, Okay.

Exeunt Elder Sister.

THE VOICE OF ELDER SISTER:

So many pajamas here, which one do you want?

YOUNGER SISTER: The one with elephant pattern.

THE VOICE OF ELDER SISTER:

Elephant···Where's the elephant···?

YOUNGER SISTER: Do you find it?

THE VOICE OF ELDER SISTER:

I'm still trying.

YOUNGER SISTER: Just the one with elephant pattern.

(Pause)

It's Okay.

THE VOICE OF ELDER SISTER:

What?

Enter Younger Sister. She goes to the backyard. Exeunt Younger Sister.

THE VOICE OF YOUNGER SISTER:

It's okay. Thanks. I can do it myself.

THE VOICE OF ELDER SISTER:

Oh. Okay.

Enter Younger Sister, holding a pink pajama. She goes directly into the bedroom.

Enter Elder Sister. She wants to look into the bedroom but younger sister closes the door.

After a while, Younger Sister comes out of the bedroom. She gently closes the door.

ELDER SISTER: She's sleeping?

YOUNGER SISTER: Yes. Finally. Sorry, I'm too busy⋯always got a mountain of dirty clothes to wash.

They sit on the sofa.

ELDER SISTER: You look tired.

YOUNGER SISTER: Well···Not really. You have to get used
                         to it. Baby at this age···quite difficult to
                         fall asleep···

ELDER SISTER: She looks like you a lot.

YOUNGER SISTER: What?

ELDER SISTER: The baby, I mean. Especially the nose.

YOUNGER SISTER: Ah, yes···but not in character···I think
                         she takes after you.

ELDER SISTER: After me? How can you tell that? She's
                         just a baby!

They laugh.

YOUNGER SISTER: Oh I forget to turn on the lights. Sorry.

*Younger Sister turns on the light. The house becomes quite
bright.*

YOUNGER SISTER: You want some water?

ELDER SISTER: Ok, thanks.

*Younger Sister gets a glass of water for Elder Sister.
Younger Sister starts to tidy up the room.*

ELDER SISTER: When did those buildings built up?

YOUNGER SISTER: What buildings?

ELDER SISTER:	Those I saw in the backyard, close to the mountains.
YOUNGER SISTER:	Ah. Just a few years ago, from the direction of train station.
ELDER SISTER:	Train station?
YOUNGER SISTER:	You don't remember? Come, I'll show you. *(They look through the window)* The station is right over there. Can you see it?
ELDER SISTER:	Ah, yes! I remember these places were rice fields in the past, when we were still kids. You could see the train station at the first glance···very big one. But it looks so small now.
YOUNGER SISTER:	And do you remember those frogs? There used to be so many frogs croaking in summer nights, so hard for me to fall asleep.
ELDER SISTER:	I really miss them.
YOUNGER SISTER:	Miss what?
ELDER SISTER:	Those frogs.
YOUNGER SISTER:	Ah, yes, frogs. *(Smile)* Croak! Croak!
ELDER SISTER:	I also saw many lights on the mountains. What are those lights? I couldn't remember.
YOUNGER SISTER:	Those are Hot Spring Hotels. It's tourist season now, business booming.
ELDER SISTER:	Ah.
YOUNGER SISTER:	You can see buses full of tourist groups going up to the mountains in the day time.
ELDER SISTER:	Hometown has changed so much, I couldn't even recognize it.

YOUNGER SISTER:	Because you've been away for so such a long time.
ELDER SISTER:	I've no choice. I'm too busy.
YOUNGER SISTER:	You've been away for ten years···
ELDER SISTER:	I have to paint···open up exhibitions. Sometimes I'll have to pack and fly to somewhere else after just a phone call.
YOUNGER SISTER:	···
ELDER SISTER:	I've asked you to come but you refused.
YOUNGER SISTER:	I couldn't afford the tickets···
ELDER SISTER:	I told you that you could···
YOUNGER SISTER:	I'm also busy. I work during the day··· sometimes I'll have to do another job at night, or take care of dad. And now, you see, I've got my baby to look after.
ELDER SISTER:	···
YOUNGER SISTER:	The house also needs someone to take care of.
ELDER SISTER:	···
YOUNGER SISTER:	Is everything ok today? Does she behave like a good girl?
ELDER SISTER:	Ah, yes. She was as good as gold. We spent the whole afternoon playing. She really loved to play with me and kept smiling at me.
YOUNGER SISTER:	Ah, that's good···
ELDER SISTER:	But she cried when I was changing her diaper··· I was in such a spin. I didn't know how to comfort her.
YOUNGER SISTER:	Don't worry. Babies always cry while doing diaper changing.
ELDER SISTER:	Hope she didn't hurt.
YOUNGER SISTER:	Actually···I feel sorry, really.

ELDER SISTER:	What?
YOUNGER SISTER:	I've got work to do, the babysitter suddenly said she couldn't come today···
ELDER SISTER:	Hey.
YOUNGER SISTER:	···
ELDER SISTER:	It's okay, really. No problem.
YOUNGER SISTER:	···
ELDER SISTER:	I love kids.
YOUNGER SISTER:	You? *(Laughs)*
ELDER SISTER:	···I know, I know···But these years things changed. Sometimes I would imagine having a baby.
YOUNGER SISTER:	You just need to take good care of yourself. Changing diapers, breast-feeding···these things are so trivial, so annoying. You can't handle it. Believe me.
ELDER SISTER:	···
YOUNGER SISTER:	Ah, I bought mochi today. Do you want some?
ELDER SISTER:	No, thanks.
YOUNGER SISTER:	Why? I thought you love it.
ELDER SISTER:	Yes, but···No, thanks. Really.
YOUNGER SISTER:	I bought it especially for you. See?
	You know that I don't eat these things. I used to suffer from diarrhea after eating mochi.
ELDER SISTER:	···
YOUNGER SISTER:	You never got a chance to eat these abroad. Come on.
ELDER SISTER:	Okay.

Elder Sister sits at the table, staring at the mochi.

Younger Sister gets another glass of water for her.

YOUNGER SISTER: What?

ELDER SISTER: No, nothing. *(Eats mochi)* Oh my god. The taste is so···Do you remember, when we in junior high school, an old man would sell mochi during the weekends near our house. You remember? You always ran behind his bicycle and fell over···

YOUNGER SISTER: Well···

ELDER SISTER: Nothing. Forget it. I mean···It tastes good.

YOUNGER SISTER: Great.

ELDER SISTER: I miss the taste so much. Feels like I'm really back home.

YOUNGER SISTER: Told you.

SCENE III

YOUNGER SISTER:	Actually, I remember that.
ELDER SISTER:	Remember what?
YOUNGER SISTER:	The old mochi man.
ELDER SISTER:	Oh—
YOUNGER SISTER:	He used to put the whole big chunk of mochi at the back of his bicycle, in a large wooden box. He would peddle it in the streets, crying, "MO—CHI! Tasting MO—CHI!" How could I forget that?
ELDER SISTER:	Yeah.
YOUNGER SISTER:	Dad used to buy a lot of mochi for you. He knew you love eating mochi.
ELDER SISTER:	Dad loved us.
YOUNGER SISTER:	Not us. He loved you. He gave you everything you wanted. Piano, ballet, English courses⋯Do you remember that one day, you showed off your piano competition medal in front of me. You told me that you went for a drive with dad in his police car. I was so envy of you at that time.
ELDER SISTER:	Come on, let bygones be bygones.
YOUNGER SISTER:	When dad bought too much mochi, you also forced me to eat, do you remember?
ELDER SISTER:	Did I?
YOUNGER SISTER:	Yes you did! You sat in front of my bed and forced me to eat. If I refused, you would feed me. Sometimes you would shovel a big chunk directly into my mouth. Don't you remember?

Younger Sister shovels the mochi into Elder Sister's mouth.

They laugh.

ELDER SISTER:	I didn't do that!
YOUNGER SISTER:	And you said that, I'm your younger sister, I must share the responsibility with you. We are the same, we are both daddy's good girls. We must share the love of him.
ELDER SISTER:	Yes, yes⋯
YOUNGER SISTER:	You also frightened me, you said that I couldn't tell dad that you forced me to eat. You said⋯you said that if I refused to eat, I would be drive away from the house just like mom.
ELDER SISTER:	Have I said those words?
YOUNGER SISTER:	Yes, you have.
ELDER SISTER:	I can't remember.

(Pause)

YOUNGER SISTER:	Have you thought that why mom didn't take us away with her?
ELDER SISTER:	Because the custody was given to dad.
YOUNGER SISTER:	I know, I know. But mom and dad could each take one of us. This would be fairer.
ELDER SISTER:	I never thought of it.

(Pause)

YOUNGER SISTER:	Actually, mom wanted to take me away with her at that time.
ELDER SISTER:	She said she wanted to leave alone.

YOUNGER SISTER:	She said she wanted to take me away.
ELDER SISTER:	No, no way.
YOUNGER SISTER:	You wouldn't know because she came to school to see me privately. She said she didn't want to go home, she didn't want to see dad.
ELDER SISTER:	But you stayed. It was your own choice.
YOUNGER SISTER:	Not me. It was your choice.
ELDER SISTER:	My choice?
YOUNGER SISTER:	You asked me to stay. Don't you remember? You told me that mom would never come back. She would have another family. She would have her own kids. You said you wanted me to accompany you··· You cried so hard at that time.
ELDER SISTER:	Did I?
YOUNGER SISTER:	I stayed. But soon you left. Ten years, you left me alone, staying with dad.
ELDER SISTER:	···
YOUNGER SISTER:	I was thinking if I left with mom at that time, maybe things would be better.
ELDER SISTER:	Maybe would be worse. Who knows?
YOUNGER SISTER:	Yeah···you're right.

SCENE IV

YOUNGER SISTER:	Are you tired?
ELDER SISTER:	Well, I···
YOUNGER SISTER:	It's a little bit late···

Younger Sister stands up.

Elder Sister stands up and fetches her coat.

ELDER SISTER:	Don't bother. I'm used to staying in hotels.
YOUNGER SISTER:	You're going to hotel?
ELDER SISTER:	Yes.
YOUNGER SISTER:	Why do you book hotel? You should stay here! I've already cleaned up your room today.
ELDER SISTER:	Room? My room?
YOUNGER SISTER:	Of course, your room on the second floor.
ELDER SISTER:	You still keep the room for me?
YOUNGER SISTER:	Come on, let me show you.

Younger Sister leads Elder Sister to the second floor.

YOUNGER SISTER:	You see, the curtains are still old ones. The furniture, the things on your table are exactly at the same place. I'll never enter this room unless I think I need to do the cleaning.
ELDER SISTER:	Thank you. But I still don't want to sleep yet. I guess I would stay awake until

tomorrow morning.

YOUNGER SISTER:	So···still no better?
ELDER SISTER:	What?
YOUNGER SISTER:	It sounded like a severe one.
ELDER SISTER:	What?
YOUNGER SISTER:	I··· I remember that one night, you couldn't sleep at night and you were arrested···
ELDER SISTER:	Ah, come on!
YOUNGER SISTER:	What?
ELDER SISTER:	I cannot sleep now because of the jet lag.
YOUNGER SISTER:	Oh, yes! Jet lag! Look at me, what am I talking about!
ELDER SISTER:	Not because of that.
YOUNGER SISTER:	I didn't mean that.
ELDER SISTER:	It's okay, never mind.
YOUNGER SISTER:	How long does it take to fly back home?
ELDER SISTER:	Almost 20 hours.
YOUNGER SISTER:	Such a long time!
ELDER SISTER:	Yes.
	I really couldn't sleep in the past.
YOUNGER SISTER:	Couldn't sleep at all?
ELDER SISTER:	Yes. It's very hard to sleep on the plane.
YOUNGER SISTER:	Ah, you mean on the plane.
ELDER SISTER:	Time and space are in such a disorder during the long flight. You cannot tell whether it's dawn or midnight. It seems that you're living in another parallel universe.

YOUNGER SISTER:	Mm···
ELDER SISTER:	But this time, I couldn't help myself. I slept like a log and I even couldn't remember how many meals I've already had. I think I've caught up on all the sleep I've missed in my whole life.
YOUNGER SISTER:	That's good···You've slept enough. That's good.
ELDER SISTER:	···Have I told you?
YOUNGER SISTER:	What?
ELDER SISTER:	I couldn't sleep···stuff.
YOUNGER SISTER:	Yes you did.
ELDER SISTER:	When?
YOUNGER SISTER:	That midnight you called me.
ELDER SISTER:	Midnight?
YOUNGER SISTER:	Yeah. Midnight. I even got no time to put on my pajamas.
ELDER SISTER:	I've no idea.
YOUNGER SISTER:	You cried on the phone.
ELDER SISTER:	I cried?
YOUNGER SISTER:	You told me you were in the police station. I was frightened to death.
ELDER SISTER:	Are you sure that was me?
YOUNGER SISTER:	Of course it was you! Who else?
ELDER SISTER:	Maybe you were dreaming.
YOUNGER SISTER:	Ok, Ok. Enough. I think I'm still able to tell the difference between dreams and real life.
ELDER SISTER:	Hey, hey. I'm Sorry. It's only a joke.
YOUNGER SISTER:	···Not funny.
ELDER SISTER:	To tell you the truth, I really couldn't remember these stuff at all.

YOUNGER SISTER:	⋯Have you already been to the doctor's?
ELDER SISTER:	Yes. But they couldn't find the reason.
YOUNGER SISTER:	⋯
ELDER SISTER:	Maybe⋯because of the screaming.
YOUNGER SISTER:	Screaming?
ELDER SISTER:	Have you heard of Edvard Munch?
YOUNGER SISTER:	Who?
ELDER SISTER:	Edvard Munch. He is a Norwegian painter. He has drawn a painting of someone screaming on a bridge. Do you know that? It's very famous.
YOUNGER SISTER:	Famous⋯? Then it must has been shown on TV⋯
ELDER SISTER:	Ah, yes. Last time on TV was the auction of this painting. It was sold.
YOUNGER SISTER:	How much?
ELDER SISTER:	One hundred and twenty million dollars, if I remember correctly.
YOUNGER SISTER:	Oh my god!
ELDER SISTER:	I've seen the authentic work in the museum of Oslo. The painting was right in front of me as if I could touch one hundred and twenty million dollars with my fingertips.
YOUNGER SISTER:	⋯
ELDER SISTER:	Anyway, the painting was so weird, you know. The sky was painted red, like the volcano eruption.
YOUNGER SISTER:	Red sky? I know. Just exactly like your painting.
ELDER SISTER:	What?
YOUNGER SISTER:	The painting you sent to me, the one with a white frame, do you remember?

ELDER SISTER:	Well, yes, they were a little bit alike...but⋯not much alike.
YOUNGER SISTER:	Mm⋯
ELDER SISTER:	I don't know why⋯by the first time I saw the painting, the guy screaming on the bridge, I started to think⋯Maybe we're the same.
YOUNGER SISTER:	⋯
ELDER SISTER:	Munch also suffered from insomnia. I thought he was also troubled by the screaming, just like me.
YOUNGER SISTER:	I don't understand⋯
ELDER SISTER:	You know what...when I went to bed one night, I suddenly heard a screaming with a high decibel scale.
YOUNGER SISTER:	Where does the screaming come from?
ELDER SISTER:	The second floor where I used to paint.
YOUNGER SISTER:	What kind of screaming?
ELDER SISTER:	It was a girl's screaming. She was crying for help.
YOUNGER SISTER:	Who is that girl?
ELDER SISTER:	I don't know so I went to the attic to see. It was empty. Nobody there but me.
YOUNGER SISTER:	⋯
ELDER SISTER:	She screamed every night. I couldn't stand any longer so I opened my window and screamed with her. Then the neighbor called the police. I was arrested and later stayed in the hospital for almost two weeks.
YOUNGER SISTER:	Have you found the reason?
ELDER SISTER:	No, because she continued to scream. She didn't stop. So I gave up. I left her alone in the attic.
YOUNGER SISTER:	So you⋯you left her there⋯?

SCENE V

ELDER SISTER:	Well then, stop talking about me. Tell me something about you.
YOUNGER SISTER:	Me? I've got nothing to say.
ELDER SISTER:	Why? You can talk about your work···
YOUNGER SISTER:	My work···nothing special, just hanging in there.
ELDER SISTER:	Aren't you busy?
YOUNGER SISTER:	Well, not really. Just stand behind the counter. It was a little bit difficult at first. The charges were always wrong so I had to pay with my own salary. But now it's much better. Ah, and sometimes I also work in the convenience store.
ELDER SISTER:	Still the counter work?
YOUNGER SISTER:	No. In convenience store we do everything.
ELDER SISTER:	Oh, okay.
YOUNGER SISTER:	I always run into strange customers or strange things working in the store.
ELDER SISTER:	Why?
YOUNGER SISTER:	Hard to say···well, okay. You know, one day while I was working in the store, a customer came to the counter with a shrimp sushi roll. I helped him to scan the barcode, but it didn't work out. So I decided to key the code. You know, everything has a code in the store. But it didn't work out either. Maybe the sushi roll was a new product, maybe there was something wrong with the barcode, or maybe the system was out of order. So

I asked the customer whether he could fetch another roll for me to scan. He said he couldn't help because this was the last one in the store. What should I do? I couldn't ask him to eat something else. I looked behind him, the other customers started to queue in just a few seconds. As usual, there would be two cashiers at the counter, but I didn't know why my colleague wasn't there at that moment. There were two young office workers standing behind him. It seemed that they were in a hurry. So I restarted the system. The queue was turning into another side of the store. I couldn't get through to my colleague so I decided to call the manager. But I suddenly realized that he was on his vacation. If I call him, he would be angry and dock my salary. The other customers started to quarrel and shout, they kept asking what was wrong. The two office workers also frowned and stamped their feet. But the customer, I mean the one with the sushi roll, he stood right in front of the counter, I knew he wouldn't leave without the shrimp sushi roll. I looked at that guy, I found out that he looked a little bit like dad. I knew that: I AM SO DEAD!

I sensed a feeling of useless for the first time in my life. I'm just so stupid.

	Then I started to cry. I kept saying: I'm sorry, I'm so sorry. My bad. My fault. Please forgive me! I AM TERRIBILY SORRY—
ELDER SISTER:	⋯Then?
YOUNGER SISTER:	⋯I couldn't really remember. I was crying so badly that day.
	Then the customers left. My colleague came back. As if nothing had happened. So I picked up the shrimp sushi roll that man left on the counter.
	Beep! Passed.
	I deleted the record and I scanned the barcode again. Beep! Passed! I tried the third time. Beep! Passed! I tried another ten times and yes, it just passed! So what happened just now? I just don't understand! It's so wired! Don't you think so?
ELDER SISTER:	Mm.
YOUNGER SISTER:	Are you listening to me?
ELDER SISTER:	Yes, yes of course.
YOUNGER SISTER:	I told you I've got nothing special to say.
ELDER SISTER:	I'm just thinking, if you don't like your job, then just quit.
YOUNGER SISTER:	I cannot do that. I'm different from you. I don't have much choice.
ELDER SISTER: ⋯	
YOUNGER SISTER:	But I love supermarket. Supermarket is different.
ELDER SISTER:	What's the difference? Both are counter jobs.

YOUNGER SISTER:	No, quite different. In super market, I can get on and off duty on time. The sound of scan machine is much more pleasant. I mean, the sound is lower, B-E-E-P···So I can do my work evenly and won't be distracted. I will not get nervous. Sometimes when the customers buy a lot of stuff, I will pull the long shopping list out of the machine. It's so satisfying! And I have a lot of colleagues in the supermarket, if I have any questions, I can just turn around and··· Wow, you can see a whole row of colleagues. You can ask any questions at any time. Ah, and we can always take part in the supermarket events. Last Christmas we got a hat of antlers. My face is small so I think I fit the hat perfectly. Supermarket is much simpler. I prefer a simple life.

(Pause)

YOUNGER SISTER:	But the business is not very good these days. The supermarket.
ELDER SISTER:	What happened?
YOUNGER SISTER:	A big shopping center opened a few months ago, next to the station. You can buy everything there, even the furniture.
ELDER SISTER:	Ah yes, I saw it yesterday.
YOUNGER SISTER:	We are losing customers. My colleagues are waiting for the hiring notice and jumping on there. It may be a little bit

	hard working in international companies but better benefits. If I stay here, I may lose my job anytime.
ELDER SISTER:	How about him? Did he pay you a visit?
YOUNGER SISTER:	Who?
ELDER SISTER:	⋯
YOUNGER SISTER:	Ah, him⋯Yes. About two months ago.
ELDER SISTER:	Why? Asking for money?
YOUNGER SISTER:	No.
ELDER SISTER:	What's his job now?
YOUNGER SISTER:	I don't know. I didn't ask.
ELDER SISTER: Y	ou can't live like this anymore.
YOUNGER SISTER:	I can handle it.
ELDER SISTER:	He is responsible for this.
YOUNGER SISTER:	⋯
ELDER SISTER:	You should take my advice at that time.
YOUNGER SISTER:	⋯
ELDER SISTER:	You shouldn't give birth to her at that time.
YOUNGER SISTER:	I think⋯you shouldn't say these words.
	The baby wanted to be born. She was on her way. You can't make up your mind for her. I think you also shouldn't judge my life.
ELDER SISTER:	I don't understand you.
YOUNGER SISTER:	Me neither, actually.
	I feel a little strange. My baby was born, and everyone suddenly appeared in my life, bustling with noise. Everyone wanted to give some advice. They kept saying that she shouldn't be born, while my baby was holding right in their arms. They also kept saying that he should

take the responsibility.

It's so weird. She is my baby. None of anyone's business. Children still can lead a good life without a father. Maybe a better life.

I said, I prefer a simple life. That's all.

SCENE VI

YOUNGER SISTER:	It's late. Do you want to go to bed?
ELDER SISTER:	Oh, okay.
YOUNGER SISTER:	I'll get you a towel.

Younger Sister goes up to the second floor.
She returns with a towel in her hand.

YOUNGER SISTER:	Here you go.
ELDER SISTER:	Thank you.
	Oh by the way, where do you put my paintings? Those I sent to you?
YOUNGER SISTER:	Oh, I put them on the second floor. The attic is now full of your paintings.
ELDER SISTER:	The second floor···
YOUNGER SISTER:	I don't know where to put them. You know, I have no taste for art.
ELDER SISTER: ···	
YOUNGER SISTER:	And you really don't need to send those paintings to me. The shipping must be quite expensive.
ELDER SISTER:	No, it's okay. Actually I've got nothing else for you except for these paintings.

(Pause)

ELDER SISTER:	So, how do you like them?
YOUNGER SISTER:	What?
ELDER SISTER:	My paintings.

YOUNGER SISTER:	Why don't you go for a bath?
ELDER SISTER:	Come on, tell me.
YOUNGER SISTER:	I'm no expert. No comment.
ELDER SISTER:	Expert? I've had enough of those experts, critics, collectors, professors··· those terms just go around and around, spin around and around, all the time.
YOUNGER SISTER:	···
ELDER SISTER:	Say something. Come on.

(Pause)

YOUNGER SISTER:	You really want me to say?
ELDER SISTER:	Yes.
YOUNGER SISTER:	Well···Mm··· Do you remember when you were in junior high school, you always got the gold award in every painting contest.
ELDER SISTER:	Mmm-Hmm.
YOUNGER SISTER:	I loved your paintings at that time. Especially that one, the raining harbor, with lots of fishing boats. Do you remember?
ELDER SISTER:	Yes, I do.
YOUNGER SISTER:	When I was looking at that picture, I had a sense of feeling that···the rain was running out of the canvas. I loved it so much.
ELDER SISTER:	You did?
YOUNGER SISTER:	And you used to draw paintings of landscapes, farmers.
ELDER SISTER:	Yes. I also drew lots of rice fields at that time.

YOUNGER SISTER:	I really love them.
ELDER SISTER:	Thanks.
YOUNGER SISTER:	···But later···things changed. I don't understand. You go abroad, you send me paintings. But all those pictures look just the same. The same suburban house, the same open window, the same man sitting behind the dining table.
ELDER SISTER:	···
YOUNGER SISTER:	What happened? You didn't used to be this way. Have I got anything wrong? Or···?
ELDER SISTER:	···
YOUNGER SISTER:	I told you I'm not an expert.
ELDER SISTER:	You are right, actually. I continued drawing the same thing since I went abroad.
YOUNGER SISTER:	You mean···you've been drawing the same thing for ten years?
ELDER SISTER:	Yes.
YOUNGER SISTER:	···
ELDER SISTER:	I've tried a hundred of times. I stood in front of the empty canvas. I took a deep breath and I said to myself: OK! From now on, I'll draw something different! Anything! But it never worked. No matter how hard I tired. No matter I draw with my eyes open or closed, that house, that scene just arises in my mind automatically.
YOUNGER SISTER:	···
ELDER SISTER:	I don't know what happened. The switch was turned on. I could also draw other

things, but it always stopped halfway.

Last year, I opened up my own exhibition in a private gallery in New York. They exhibited my house series. Twelve pictures all together. I could still remember the opening day, it was raining. A little boy came to the gallery with his mother. I could still remember his sweet face. He went around in the gallery and then stood at the corner, staring at my paintings. I wanted to know what he saw, so I went up and asked him: "What do you see?"

He pointed at the man in the painting: "Who's this guy?"

"He is daddy." I said.

All of a sudden he turned around and asked me: "Where're the other guys? If daddy's here, where're the other family members? Do they still live in this house?"

That was what he said to me.

YOUNGER SISTER:	Why're you telling me these?

(Pause)

ELDER SISTER:	Actually I have something to discuss with you this time.
YOUNGER SISTER:	What?
ELDER SISTER:	Father's heritage.
YOUNGER SISTER:	Heritage? I thought we've already reached an agreement before you went abroad.
ELDER SISTER:	Yes, I know.

YOUNGER SISTER:	He didn't left so much. Just cashes in two bankbooks and several stocks. He divided them into two, one for you and one for me.
ELDER SISTER:	I know that.
YOUNGER SISTER:	So what's the problem?
ELDER SISTER:	He also left this house for us.
YOUNGER SISTER:	⋯
ELDER SISTER:	I guess the house is registered under our names.
YOUNGER SISTER:	Yes.
ELDER SISTER:	I'm just thinking, the house is too big. Now you live alone, sometimes you may feel lonely.
YOUNGER SISTER:	So you mean⋯

Elder Sister nods.

Younger Sister stands up and sits in the sofa.

YOUNGER SISTER:	You are just so selfish.
ELDER SISTER:	No, you listen to me. I know you love here, I know for you, this is the best place in the world. But I'm just so different from you—
YOUNGER SISTER:	Yes, you are right. We're so different from each other.
	You open up your exhibition abroad, flying from one place to another. You go to London, Paris, Tokyo and San Francisco⋯Places I've never even dreamed of. How about me? I guess I would spend rest of my life staying here forever, in this small town, in this old house.

ELDER SISTER: I didn't mean that.

YOUNGER SISTER: I took care of dad all these years. He
                       kept asking me, "Where's your sister?
                       When would she come back?" I didn't
                       know how to answer him. He passed
                       away and you didn't even call back. I
                       arranged all the funeral all by myself.

                       Now you come back and the only thing
                       you want is to divide the family wealth
                       with me. I don't understand.

ELDER SISTER: You misunderstand me.

YOUNGER SISTER: Look at you. You just want to do
                       whatever you like. You make decisions
                       for others and we have no choice but to
                       obey you. Who gives you the right to do
                       this?

ELDER SISTER: ...

YOUNGER SISTER: I will never sell this house.

*Younger Sister takes the luggage of Elder Sister and goes up
to the second floor.*

Elder Sister is left alone in the living room.

Younger Sister returns.

YOUNGER SISTER: Forget about it. From now on, we keep
                       lead our own lives. When's your plane
                       tomorrow?

ELDER SISTER: But I don't want to paint any more.

YOUNGER SISTER: What?

ELDER SISTER: Painting the houses. I've had enough.

YOUNGER SISTER: I don't understand you.

Younger Sister goes into the bedroom.

ELDER SISTER: The house has three floors. The top floor
has a high ceiling with wood decorations.
The first floor has a fish tank and a big
crystal chandelier. The window is always
open, all the year round. Every time
when I came back from school, I could
see the lights went though from the
window. I knew dad was still awake. He
was waiting for me.

(Pause)

That day, I went back home as usual. I
opened the door of the second floor. So
quiet, so quiet that I could only hear a
small sound. It was the fish tank filter.
Then I saw dad. He was standing in
the corridor. He said, "Hey you. Come
here."

He had always been like this. He taught
us to listen to his words. We must do
everything he asked us to do. We didn't
dare to say no. He spoke with a cold and
short voice, as if he was giving orders to
his subordinates.

Younger Sister goes out of the bedroom.

YOUNGER SISTER: Can you keep your voice down?
I'm tired. I want to go to bed.

Younger Sister turns off the lights. Dim light.
She sleeps on the sofa.

ELDER SISTER:	I didn't dare to say no. So I went up and sat beside him. I could smell alcohol in his breath. He said to me: "Now lie down." I couldn't move. I could just see the small yellow star on his shoulder. I was a little bit nervous because I hadn't finished my homework…Suddenly the star started to move…I felt pain. I wanted to scream with fear. I wanted to call for help. But he said, "Shut up. If you make any noise, I will drive you out of this house, just like your mother."
YOUNGER SISTER:	…
ELDER SISTER:	The next day, I saw a pack of mochi on the dining table. He bought it for me.
	You know what…when the little boy asked me, "Where're the other guys in this house?" I didn't know what to say. Yes, why didn't I thought of it? At that time, I was left alone with him. What about you? Where were the other guys?
	That day I got back to my studio. I saw those paintings in my attic. All the space was stuffed with this house, this window…and this man. I suddenly felt so tired.
	I'm just so tired. I don't want to paint any more.
YOUNGER SISTER:	…
ELDER SISTER:	The only solution is to sell the house. I don't come for money. I just don't want to have any simple tiny connection with this house. I want to delete my memory and start a new life!
	Do you understand me?

SCENE VII

Younger Sister goes up and turns on the light.

She stands in front of the dining room table.

She starts to eat mochi.

YOUNGER SISTER: He also bought this for me at that time.

ELDER SISTER: What?

YOUNGER SISTER: Mochi. This is dad's gift. He would buy mochi for good girl.

ELDER SISTER: ···What?

YOUNGER SISTER: But I couldn't eat at all. I just couldn't.

ELDER SISTER: He···he also bought this for YOU?

YOUNGER SISTER: How did you manage to eat?

ELDER SISTER: ···Do you hear that?

YOUNGER SISTER: What?

ELDER SISTER: The baby···baby is crying.

YOUNGER SISTER: I hear nothing.

I'm asking you. How did you manage to eat?

ELDER SISTER: Why didn't you tell me at that time?

YOUNGER SISTER: Nothing would change.

ELDER SISTER: We could call the police! We could···

YOUNGER SISTER: Dad was a policeman. Do you think they would trust you or trust dad?

ELDER SISTER: We should···we could find a solution! We are sisters, we could find a solution!

YOUNGER SISTER: What about you? Why didn't you tell me then?

ELDER SISTER: I···I just···

YOUNGER SISTER:	Come on, you would never call the police. You got the goods and you could frighten dad, then you could do anything you want.
ELDER SISTER:	What are you talking about?
YOUNGER SISTER:	You could do anything you want. You took everything for granted! How about me? You would never think of me. I knew···I knew this for a long time that you···you believed that···dad would never have any interest in me. Did I say something wrong?
ELDER SISTER:	···
YOUNGER SISTER:	Dad loved you so much. He didn't want you to leave.
ELDER SISTER:	Stop···stop saying these···
YOUNGER SISTER:	You threatened dad before you leave, didn't you? Dad told me everything. He said that, if he didn't let you go at that time, you would···you would···
ELDER SISTER:	···
YOUNGER SISTER:	I'm not as clever as you···
ELDER SISTER:	···
YOUNGER SISTER:	After so many years did I realize that··· that I'm just a substitute for you.
ELDER SISTER:	He treated me so well but I felt so bad. But I had no choice.
YOUNGER SISTER:	It's Okay. It's Okay.
ELDER SISTER:	I really don't know what happened to you···
YOUNGER SISTER:	It's Okay. Forget it. Let's just pretend that nothing happened.

SCENE VIII

ELDER SISTER: How about you? How did you manage it?

YOUNGER SISTER: What?

ELDER SISTER: How did you manage to forget?

YOUNGER SISTER: I did nothing. I just wait.

ELDER SISTER: Wait?

YOUNGER SISTER: I waited and waited. Until he became old, until one day he fell down on the floor and fainted, until he lied in bed and couldn't even wipe his own butt. I waited until he begged me, until he said, "Please help me, please have some mercy⋯" I knew this day would come. I did nothing. I just wait.

ELDER SISTER: ⋯

YOUNGER SISTER: He died. The house is mine now. Nobody would enter without my permission. I don't want to go anywhere after work, I just want to come back home.

And him⋯yes, actually you're right. Several months ago, he did came for money. But I don't care. He could get as much as he wanted as long as he kept a distance from my baby. I really don't care. But he will never enter this house.

ELDER SISTER: ⋯The house is just so old. It will become more and more expensive in the future. Have you really never had a thought of⋯

YOUNGER SISTER: YOU SHUT UP!

SCENE IX

ELDER SISTER: I flew back to New York the next day. I didn't say goodbye to her.

Two years later, London Museum opened an exhibition for me. They exhibited my house series. Forty-six altogether. That was my biggest individual exhibition and it was such a success. I remember there was an art critic saying that:

"···Those paintings even exceed Edvard Munch, showing a sense of distorted repeatability. The anxiety booms out of the simple colors and lines, reflecting the imbalance of contemporary society which attacked by existence.

Really? I don't even know that···

People will just remember the price of Munch's painting. One hundred and twenty million dollars. But nobody could remember the reason why would he drew that screaming.

I had to answer lots of phone calls. Trucks came to my studio and carried my paintings away to more and more places. The invisible little girl in my paintings still continued her silent screaming. The collectors kept asking me: "When will you draw a new piece?"

But the scream stopped.

I could never paint the house any more.

Younger Sister goes back to the bedroom.

SCENE X

Elder Sister spoke with Younger Sister through the door.

ELDER SISTER: It's too late. I should go.

THE VOICE OF YOUNGER SISTER:
        Oh, Okay.

ELDER SISTER: She's sleeping soundly.

THE VOICE OF YOUNGER SISTER:
        Yeah.

ELDER SISTER: She is so sweet. Bye-bye, Bye-bye.

THE VOICE OF YOUNGER SISTER:
        Will you come tomorrow?

ELDER SISTER: Yeah, I guess so. When will you get off work tomorrow?

THE VOICE OF YOUNGER SISTER:
        I work the night shift tomorrow.

ELDER SISTER: Do you need me to take care of her?

THE VOICE OF YOUNGER SISTER:
        Oh, no. Thank you.

ELDER SISTER: Really?

THE VOICE OF YOUNGER SISTER:
                          For real.

ELDER SISTER: Then···Goodbye.

THE VOICE OF YOUNGER SISTER:
                          Goodbye.

ELDER SISTER: Goodnight.

The lights goes off all of a sudden.

-THE END-

《姊妹》

二〇一六年十一月三日
首演於台北牯嶺街小劇場，
盜火劇團主辦及演出。

編　　劇：劉天涯
導　　演：蘇洋徵
藝術總監：謝東寧
製 作 人：劉天涯
專案製作：楊名芝
舞台暨服裝設計：趙鈺涵
燈光設計：蘇揚清
聲音設計：許博丞
視覺設計暨攝影：葛昌惠
舞台監督：曾智偉
執行製作：黃澄閑、沈琬婷
CF導演攝影暨剪輯：楊博達

演　　員：王渝婷 飾 姐姐
　　　　　林唐聿 飾 妹妹

photo credit：葛昌惠

劇作家簡介

photo credit：葛昌惠

劉天涯，1991年生於江蘇徐州，南京大學戲劇影視文學系畢，國立臺北藝術大學劇場藝術創作研究所（劇本創作組）。台灣盜火劇團駐團劇作家。所作舞台劇曾於中國大陸、加拿大、台灣、日本、馬來西亞等地演出。創作亦涵括小說、散文、繪本故事等。

BRIEF INTRODUCTION OF PLAYWRIGHT

LIU Tianya was born in 1991, Jiangsu, China. Playwright and novelist. Playwright-in-residency of Voleur du Feu Theatre. She was graduated from Nanjing University and is now further studying in the Department of Theatre, Taipei National University of the Arts (TNUA), major in playwriting.

劇作家作品

《浮士德3》　　　　與德國康斯坦茨應用技術大學藝術創作部合作，加拿大蒙
特羅國際劇場藝術節、南京市青春劇場，2012。

《複‧速》　　　　與壞鞋子舞蹈劇場合作，擔任文本創作，馬來西亞
Damansara Performing Arts Center，2013。

《茱莉小姐》　　　文本改編，日本鈴木忠志利賀青年導演競賽，2013。

《買四送一》　　　盜火劇團，華山1914藝文中心果酒禮堂、高雄衛武營，
2014；嘉義表演藝術中心實驗劇場口碑加演，2015。

《美麗小巴黎》　　盜火劇團，台南藝術節原生劇場、台北牯嶺街小劇場、南
京大學仙林黑匣子劇場、杭州新遠木馬劇場四地巡迴演
出23場，2015。北京9劇場行動劇場─廣藝兩岸小劇場藝術
節，2016。

《歸來吧！iminami na pazay》
玄奘大學影劇藝術學系暨原住民學士專班學年製作，
2015。

180

《玩命諾拉》　　　文本改編，國立台北藝術大學戲劇學院冬季公演，2015。

《那邊的我們》　　盜火劇團，台北牯嶺街小劇場，南京大學仙林黑匣子劇場，揚州青麥坊黑匣子劇場—江蘇原創小劇場戲劇雙年展、上海1933微劇場—上海當代戲劇節，2016。

《姊妹》　　　　　盜火劇團，台北牯嶺街小劇場—第一屆自己的劇本原創戲劇節，2016。

MAIN THEATRE WORKS
OF PLAYWRIGHT

- FAUST 3 (Playwright, 2012)

  Les Fêtes Internationales du théâtre, Montreal, Canada, in collaboration with the Theatre Institute of Nanjing University (China) and Konstanz University of Applied Sciences (Germany)

- La Vitesse Complexe (Complex Velocity),(Text, 2013)

  In collaboration with Damansara Performing Arts Centre (Malaysia)

- Miss Julie (Script Adaptation, 2013)

  Participated in Asia Theatre Directors' Festival TOGA (Japan)

- Buy Four and Get One Free (Playwright, 2014)

  Staged in Taipei, Kaohsiung and Chiayi, with Voleur du Feu Theatre.

- Le Petit Paris (Playwright, 2015-2016)

  Staged in Tainan, Taipei, Nanjing, Hangzhou and Beijing, with Voleur du Feu Theatre.

- Iminami na pazay (Playwright, 2015), staged in Hsinchu.

- Nora Kills (Script Adaptation, 2015), staged in Taipei.

- Ici·Là-bas (Playwright, 2016), staged in Taipei, Nanjing, Yangzhou and Shanghai with Voleur du Feu Theatre.

- Le Cri (Playwright, 2016), staged in Taipei, with Voleur du Feu Theatre.

盜火劇團簡介

盜火劇團由藝術總監謝東寧於2013年創立。劇團取名「盜火」，是效法普羅米修斯盜火造福人類，盜火劇團企圖以劇場力量，走入人群、影響社會。

在創作方面，主要開發本土觀點的新創作，亦以導演的總體劇場觀念，詮釋當代新文本及世界經典劇作，期待透過劇場，能夠反映社會真實、土地情感，期待以全球的視野觀看，華人生活的劇場圖像。盜火劇團亦肩負「藝術教育及社區推廣」、「劇團海外交流」、「文化政策研究」…等工作。

BRIEF INTRODUCTION OF
VOLEUR DU FEU THEATRE

Voleur du Feu Theatre was founded in 2013 by Artistic Director Hsieh Tung Ning.

The name of the company was inspired by the Greek myth, which Prometheus stole fire from Zeus in order to benefit human beings, aiming to bring the warmth through theatre works into public.

Voleur du Feu Theatre predominantly focuses on producing new creations with ethnic Chinese perspectives, New Writing plays, and adaption of classical scripts from contemporary perspectives, aiming to respond to territory, emotion, identity and social reality. The artistic approach of the company has attempted to integrate the trend of world theatre, presenting the company rooted in locality yet shaped by global vision.

盜火原創劇目（劇作者）（2014～2016）

劉天涯：《買四送一》、《美麗小巴黎》、《那邊的我們》、《姊妹》

蘇洋徵：《電台屍令》、《圖書館戰爭：特洛伊》、《電台屍令II：終戰屋》

何應權：《請讓我進去》、《海馬與象》

胡錦筵：《颱風走在預報前》

傅凱羚：《蔚然》

盜火劇團網站
WEBSITE OF VOLEUR DU FEU THEATRE

www.facebook.com/voleurdufeu.theatre

信箱
E-MAIL

voldufeu@gmail.com

Voleur du Feu Theatre [Sinophone Play Lab] I
Ici·Là-bas & Le Cri

Author	*LIU Tianya*
Translator	*LIU Tianya*
Editor	*HSIEH Tung-Ning*
Designer	*HUANG Cheng-Shian*
Published by	*Voleur du Feu Theatre*
E-mail	*voldufeu@gmail.com*
Website	*www.facebook.com/voleurdufeu.theatre*
Price	*NT. 240*

February, 2017
ISBN:978-986-94396-0-2

Copyright © LIU Tianya, 2017

All rights reserved. No part of this publication may be
reproduced, utilized or transmitted in any form or by any
means, electronic or mechanical, including photocopy,
recording, or any information storage and retrieval system,
without permission in writing from the publisher.

VOLEUR DU FEU THEATRE
11257 4F, No. 5, Ln.168, Sec 3, Zhongyang N. Rd, Beitou
Dist, Taipei City, Taiwan (R.O.C)

國家圖書館出版品預行編目(CIP)資料

盜火劇團(華文劇本 Lab).I,<<那邊的我們>><<姊妹
>> / 劉天涯作.翻譯. -- 臺北市 : 盜火劇團,
2017.01
面 ; 公分
ISBN 978-986-94396-0-2(平裝)

854.6   106001374

盜火劇團〔華文劇本Lab〕I --《那邊的我們》《姊妹》
Voleur du Feu Theatre〔Sinophone Play Lab〕I -- Ici·Là-bas & Le Cri

作　　者：劉天涯

翻　　譯：劉天涯

主　　編：謝東寧

美術設計：黃澄閑

出版發行：盜火劇團
　　　　　11257臺北市北投區中央北路三段168巷5號4樓

電子信箱：voldufeu@gmail.com

網　　址：www.facebook.com/voleurdufeu.theatre

電　　話：02-2305-0141

郵撥帳號：第一銀行 北投分行 19110075933 戶名：盜火劇團

出版日期：2017年2月

定　　價：240元

I S B N　：978-986-94396-0-2（平裝）

欲利用、演出本書全部或部分內容者，需徵得盜火劇團書面授權。

詳情請洽盜火劇團：voldufeu@gmail.com